[signature]

Los Angeles
April 1986

The Role of the Internal Consultant

The Role of the
Internal Consultant

**Effective Role-Shaping
for Staff Positions**

Fritz Steele

VNR VAN NOSTRAND REINHOLD COMPANY
New York

To my wife, Debbie Jones-Steele

Copyright © 1982 by Van Nostrand Reinhold Company Inc.

Library of Congress Catalog Card Number: 84-7410
ISBN: 0-442-28071-8

Manufactured in the United States of America

Published by Van Nostrand Reinhold Company Inc.
135 West 50th Street
New York, New York 10020

Van Nostrand Reinhold Company Limited
Molly Millars Lane
Wokingham, Berkshire RG11 2PY, England

Van Nostrand Reinhold
480 Latrobe Street
Melbourne, Victoria 3000, Australia

Macmillan of Canada
Division of Canada Publishing Corporation
164 Commander Boulevard
Agincourt, Ontario M1S 3C7, Canada

15 14 13 12 11 10 9 8 7 6 5 4 3

Library of Congress Cataloging in Publication Data

Steele, Fritz.
  The role of the internal consultant.

  Reprint. Originally published: Boston, Mass. : CBI
Pub. Co., c1982
  Includes index.
  1. Business consultants.   I. Title.
[HD69.C6S74 1984]   658.4'6   84-7410
ISBN 0-442-28071-8

Contents

Chapter

Assumptions and
Patterns in
Internal Consulting

Today's work organization is in a continual state of transition as the world around it grows less stable. National and world economic conditions can change in a matter of months; institutional power, such as that of government regulatory agencies, has increasingly become a fact of life for U.S. companies. The type of problems which arise in maintaining a viable organization vary and their character can change fairly rapidly. A rigidly structured system, built to deal with only known or predictable problems, will find itself increasingly subject to the forces around it, with members wondering why they are ineffective even when they follow the usual channels and procedures. The costs and requirements for business are now related as much to flexibility, adaptability, and quick problem-solving as they are to discipline, order, and standardization.

As a result, there is an increased need for external consultants, because it has become harder for an organization to build up the internal resources (specialized skills and knowledge) to solve complex technical problems. For areas in which the internal resources do exist, there is an increasing demand for flexibility of deployment, with specialized people serving as internal consultants rather than limiting their responsibilities to managing a given unit. In addition, many line managers are now being asked, on a part time basis, to share their special skills or knowledge with other members of the organization. As a result, many people who are not called "consultants" are still *doing consulting* for some significant percentage of their work week. This role change tests their ability to function in new modes: providing rather than receiving services; selling their services as opposed to giving orders to subordinates; and helping someone else to do something instead of doing it themselves.

Internal consulting is, therefore, an organization's solution in dealing with specialized problems without permanently restaffing each line unit. It is a particularly apt solution when the special skills are only needed periodically in any given line unit, or when the problems cut across traditional sub-unit boundaries within the organization. These situations call for using these resources on a speedy, flexible basis wherever they are needed.

The importance of these consulting activities will continue to increase as economic and societal forces remain in flux. There will be an increasing cadre of people who are called internal consultants—specialists in information systems, financial planning and control, personnel, labor relations, engineering, law, organization development, materials management, safety, and health maintenance. Therefore, organizations increasingly will need to treat such consulting as a professional skill area, and to help employee-consultants become better able to help one another.

This need conflicts with the typical stance toward internal consulting which assumed that having an area of specialized expertise automatically made one a resource to other people. We now have plenty of evidence for the view that *knowing* a subject is not necessarily a sufficient requisite for *helping others* to deal with problems. Just as good specialists are not necessarily good teachers, good specialists are not necessarily good consultants. Helping others is a skill in itself, and poor performance for many internal staff groups does not depend on what they *know*, but, rather, on what they can't *do* in terms of the process. And, unfortunately, training and development activities are usually aimed at updating one's technical knowledge, not at improving the processes one uses for transferring that knowledge.

Another gap in present treatment of internal consulting is the lack of attention to the special forces that operate on someone who is trying to help others inside an organization. Internal consultants are subject to different demands and constraints than external ones. Understanding these forces and how to manage them creatively can mean the difference between an irritating, thankless work life and one that feels vital and stimulating.

Because of these special forces, internal consultants often face a very mixed bag of situations. This is because they tend to:

- have no direct authority over the processes and people they are supposed to influence;
- operate under ambiguous performance measures, especially as compared to line managers;
- work in units that wield little power when dealing with the larger organization;
- be squeezed by demands made on them simultaneously by different user groups, all of whom they are supposed to "serve" in order to justify their corporate existence;
- generate feelings of competitiveness in their "clients," so that they get less than hearty cooperation;
- be seen as less credible than outside consultants who may have the same (or fewer) skills;
- be put in a conflict-laden dual role of helping a unit and simultaneously checking up on it as an agent of corporate headquarters.

One main intent for this book, then, is to explore the broader view of the functions and roles of those who provide help to others within work organizations. Their labels may vary, but the expectations which surround their role provide a common focus for analysis. My aim is to reveal and explain these role problems so that they can be diagnosed and changed rather than tolerated. The overall goal, then, is to improve our skill at helping others, and so be of greater effect in our specialty.

The basic assumption throughout this book is that part time internal consultants need *increased professionalism*. This professionalism is indicated by two attitudes toward work roles: (1) a real curiosity about how you do things (to accompany the natural curiosity about a field of expertise), and (2) a commitment and regular effort to *learn* from experiences with people who are in client roles. The curiosity leads to more questions about your role and how it is shaped, and the learning focus also leads to more questions for client and colleagues about the effects (both intended and unintended) the consultant has had.

In order to help readers think clearly about role issues in the internal consulting process, I have concentrated on four basic conceptual themes:

A Process Focus

As already mentioned, I am considering internal consulting to be a *process*, not solely a position. It is something you are doing whether or not you are called a "consultant." It is worthwhile to think of consulting processes as having a finite life, that is, beginning, middle, and end phases, each of which have particular problems and opportunities. Thinking of a project as a process helps you to engage in consistent activities with a client system.

Using Role Analysis

The fields of social psychology and the applied behavioral sciences include a good deal of role analysis in social systems: what they are, how they are defined, problems caused by role conflict or ambiguity, and how roles can be changed to better achieve system goals and personal satisfaction. I believe that internal consultants are particularly susceptible to role conflict and ambiguity. Using role concepts to understand and influence experiences is one way to keep us from over-personalizing difficulties, which are usually not just our own fault. Such problems are often also the product of structures and role definitions.

Understanding Social System Dynamics

Another aid to seeing our experiences in perspective is to look at the social systems in which we are trying to do our work. Everyone obviously does this to some degree (such as learning how to play the game in your particular organization), but often without much solid background in social system dynamics. Our approach here relates to two aspects of social systems: (a) as a *context* for action, where the roles you play are embedded in and influenced by the wider social system; and (b) as a *target* for action, because what you do as an internal consultant potentially affects the social system. Many staff people think that the impact of their work is related only to their circumscribed area and tend to be unaware of the potential for widespread consequences.

Personal Influence Methods

While the focus on systems helps us to understand *what* we're influencing, looking at personal methods helps us to understand and choose *how* we can affect others. A good deal of the work laid out for an internal consultant is concerned with encouraging other people to listen, to question, to pick up an issue and run with it, or to implement a solution. Good ideas by themselves are not enough; somebody has to be willing to follow up or internal consultants will have very little impact. Chapter 8 describes a well-developed system for looking at different styles of personal influence and suggests ways to adopt more than one mode.

Internal consultants who pay attention to these themes in their work will be more likely to control their organizational fate. They will be engaged in active *role-shaping*, rather than waiting for this to be done by those around them, and so reduce the incidence of things happening "to" them. Such a role study provides legitimacy for actions that otherwise would be continually justified and explained. The themes of process, role, system, and influence provide a focus for role-shaping.

These four main themes are summarized by the diagram in Figure 1.1. In addition to these themes, there are a number of key assumptions which underlie the main text.

- Uncertainty and ambiguity are a natural, normal part of the role of an internal consultant. As such they can be limitations, but they can also be useful opportunities if they are managed well.

- Measurements of the effect that a consultant has had are often vague or fuzzy. They may conflict with one another,

Figure 1.1. Themes for the Role of the Internal Consultant

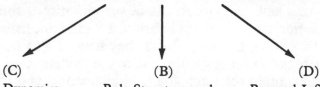

(A)

Consulting is a process which is helped
if the consultant consciously defines
his or her steps.

This Process Is Affected by Three Main Components:

(C)	(B)	(D)
Systems Dynamics and Structure:	Role Structure and Definitions:	Personal Influence and Style:
The context in which consultants work; the entity affected by their actions.	Expectations held by the consultant and "client" about what the consultant should do.	Behaviors which determine how effective such attempts are.

or be so delayed that it is hard to know what has specifically resulted from consultant efforts.

- When you are functioning as an internal consultant, you are called upon to make many choices about action, timing, and focus of your work that are not guided by policies or job descriptions. It is a good thing to make these choices as consciously as possible, rather than pursuing an action without considering other choices.

- Diagnosis, an underused activity in most consultants' repertoires, should be expanded into a consistent element. Such diagnosis includes collecting information and analyzing the causes of problems in two areas: the technical problem about which you are helping a client and your own process of working with the client. Problems can occur in either area, but most internal consultants do not generally apply diagnostic skills to their process of communication.

- Most people spend their professional energy fixing events, not on improving patterns of action. However, if you can, it is more effective to change the *patterns* of how you do your work rather than focus only on single *events*.

The main themes and assumptions thus far presented will be discussed in greater detail in the following chapters. I hope that this book will stimulate readers to practice new behaviors, look for patterns as of yet unnoticed, and seek information from the people around them concerning the ways they work and the effects they have. I also hope that my ideas and examples will speak to the readers' experiences and will contain the interest and excitement that is inherent in the internal consulting role.

Internal Consulting
as a Process

One of the prerequisites for shaping your role as an internal consultant is recognizing that you are always involved in a *process*. Regardless of what ideas, information, or products you provide, there is a shape to the way in which you do it, as well as room for considerable variation. Every effective consultant needs to be as aware of the process of helping as of the content of the help.

To this end, it is useful to think of a given consulting project as a *flow of events in time*. This flow has a beginning, a middle, and an end; and each of these stages tends to have characteristic issues, with distinct problems and opportunities. There are many ways to describe the flow process that is used by consultants. One model that is particularly useful is the seven-stage model developed by David Kolb and Alan Frohman,[1] shown summarized in Figure 2.1. Although this flow model was developed as a generalized picture of the external consulting process, it is worth briefly describing the stages for what they suggest about internal consulting. Also, its authors did not intend this to be a rigid, lockstep process where each stage neatly follows the other. In practice, there may be considerable overlap and looping, such as going back from a planning process to contract with more appropriate primary clients. The stages are meant to be approximations.

Scouting

This is the beginning of any consulting project, although it is often not recognized as being part of the process. At this stage, neither client nor consultant are committed to each other, but they are trying to find out if a helping relationship would be useful and viable. For internal consultants, scouting information can come from many sources: asking people what they know about the potential client(s), watching the potential client's behavior in public settings, such as departmental meetings or conferences, and talking informally with members in the potential client group. The consultant reviews the rumors and tidbits of information that form the basis for impressions of the client.

The client is generally conducting the same investigation about the potential consultant: trying to find out more about his reputation in the company, what he has done in

Figure 2.1. The Kolb-Frohman Model of the Consulting Process

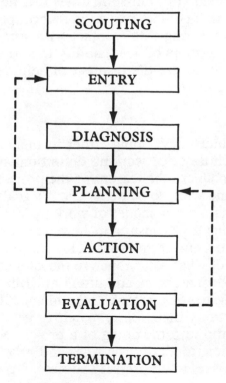

the past, and what is his style of operating. The point to remember is that all information "counts" in scouting, not just that which you get in formal meetings between client and consultant. One of the unique features of internal consulting is that the accumulation of potentially useful scouting information is always occurring, for both client and consultant, in their daily life in the organization. That is why initial meetings almost always include already ascertained opinions rather than the relatively clean slate of an external consultant attending an exploratory meeting.

One of the key questions for the consultant during scouting should be, who is the actual client for this project? Who needs the help, can support the work I do, and can use the results in a timely manner? It is often the person (or group) who has contacted you, but sometimes it is not. In this case, when the initial contact person is inappropriate, you need to establish the long-term contact with someone else. The preceding questions of need, ability to support your work, and capacity to use the results can help decide who is the appropriate client.

Entry

This stage includes developing either formal or informal contracts which describe working definitions of the problems or issues which are the reason for the project, the nature and scope of the work to be done, client's goals, the time frame, approximate costs, modes of working, expectations that either the clients or consultants have, and how the project will be evaluated and terminated. This contract sets the context for much of what will happen in the later stages, so it pays to give it adequate time and attention. But both clients (who are trying to solve a problem) and consultants (who define their worth by their ability to help or get things done) may tend to jump into the doing of a project before they have taken the time to clarify the roles and relationships that will be necessary to the project's success. A premature attack on the problem may feel like real action, but such action is often misdirected, or conducted without enough attention to long-range goals.

Diagnosis

This stage is devoted to becoming more concrete about the client's technical needs, the history of the problem, the blocks which made resolution impossible and have led to the need for outside help, and the client's resources. It is also useful to focus on underlying causes of the problem, seeing it in the context of a system of forces rather than as an isolated occurrence or need. Another area for diagnosis, which may be given short shrift by technical specialists, is an analysis of the positive and negative factors which might affect the consulting process. This is important because having a good feel for what you want your process to be will have as great a bearing on the success of the project as will a brilliant diagnosis of the technical problem. It is, nonetheless, easy for specialists to be seduced by their own interest in the problem area and to forget that they need to shape consciously both what they do and how they do it.

Diagnosis at this stage should also consider whether you have the resources to deal with the client's problems, and whether someone else should be included. Although this may sound a bit stupid, like giving away business, the internal consultant needs to promote trust. A consultant cannot just find those problems and needs for which she happens to have the solutions.

Planning

During the planning stage, the project is developed in greater detail. You decide who is to serve in what capacity, how much time you have, checkpoints, as well as alternative approaches and methods to solving the problem It is very important that this planning be done together by consultant and client, so that they both feel committed to following the plan and making it work. I have seen many internal consulting projects wither and die because the consultants did all the planning. The plans did not address the client's needs, or make the client an integral part of the process.

The plans should also include checkpoints to evaluate the progress of the project, make corrections, and if necessary, revise the basic format.

Action

This stage, of actually doing the work, is what many consultants consider "real" consultation. It should be clear by now, however, that all seven phases require "action," and that each phase can affect the outcome of the project. At this point, it is important to treat any unexpected problems and to do so as part of the normal process. That is, work methods should include how to make adjustments in a natural manner by maintaining an even keel, not an atmosphere of crisis which calls into question the basis for the consulting relationship.

Evaluation

At some point conclusions must be drawn about the value of the project and what has been produced. Is it finished? Has the time been worthwhile? How effective has the process been? Should another phase be planned? This stage is often problematic because of the difficult and mixed feelings people have about evaluating either their colleagues' or their own efforts. This part of the process goes best if it has already been planned into the project. When will we evaluate? Who will do it? What criteria will we use? How will we account for disagreement? What will we do with the results of our evaluation? If there is early agreement on these points, an evaluation can proceed smoothly and without discord.

Termination

This last stage reflects a decision made by either consultant or client or both that the project should end. This may be because the project achieved its goals or because its goals are unlikely to be achieved.

These seven stages provide a useful vehicle for making sense out of many consulting dilemmas that are difficult to decipher and resolve unless we have a sense of where we are in the process. That is, an action that would make little sense to a client and just be alienating at the beginning of a project, such as your refusal to write a particular report, might be a stroke of genius as a way of dramatizing an issue in the mutual evaluation and termination process.

However, by and large, in practical application, I have found that the seven-stage model is too elaborate, especially in light of the wide variety of work roles in today's organizations. Some groups have very little diagnosing activity, some have little formal planning, and others are limited by time. In my work with internal consultants I use a collapsed version, consisting of three stages: starting, middle, and ending. Not linguistically dazzling, perhaps, or theoretically novel, but it keeps us focused on the key consulting role issues in each phase.

Starting Phase

As already noted, the climate in which opening dialogue occurs affects everything which follows; the seeds for future opportunities, accomplishments, and difficulties are sown in the early stage of a new consulting relationship. It is important to use all that you know about the client when scouting a situation. It's also important to help the client learn about you, as a boost to his or her own scouting process. This information should include something about you as a *person*, not just your technical skills and position in the organization. It is tempting to jump right into the problems, and, in so doing, stunt the relationship-building process.

Defining the appropriate client is a key issue, and one that is not automatically decided by working with whomever you spoke with first. Defining the mode of working, the role expectations, and the ways in which these expectations can be questioned or reviewed are all seminal to the contracting process, but only once a viable definition of the client has been reached. It is particularly important to *do* this contracting, even if you have been told that it has already been done, by, for example, your group's manager and the client's manager. At the very least, you should review what commitments have been made and whether you or your client can accept them or would prefer to renegotiate on your own terms. If you want to have a consciously managed project, you should always be part of the initial contract, even if only informally. It is a mistake to assume that you're all on the same track.

You should also be very clear about what you expect from the client. What kind of help or effort do you expect and when? The tendency at the beginning is to focus on the *client's* expectations of the consultant. The consultant, then, misses the best opportunity to establish a basis for making necessary demands. This is not always a major issue, but when it is, part of your professional credibility is established by having some standards, just as external consultants do, for the client's contribution to a project. One of the reasons that external consultants are often accorded more respect than similarly skilled internal people is that outsiders are unabashed about stating *their* expectations, while internal people get into a "service" mentality which blocks them from thinking of themselves as equal partners in a contract.

Clearly, an important part of this early time is a discussion of respective roles and how these roles may be reviewed and changed during the life of the project. If this possibility, that there will be changes, is as explicit as the starting roles themselves, then whatever adjustments are made will be part of "normal" business. If, however, the notion of role revision is not clear, then any attempts in this direction will be seen as a result of major problems. Consequently, it will be much harder to talk honestly about concerns and alternatives.

Similarly, the contracting should clarify expectations about performance measures, milestones, progress reports to the client, and the kinds of regular reactions and observations which the consultant wants from the client. Being explicit about the need for client feedback sets the tone in which each of you may learn from the experience.

(The entry process is particularly tricky when you have been sent by high-level executives to troubleshoot in some subordinate unit of the organization. When you are ordered to "go help them get themselves straightened out," it is very important to do a conscious contracting effort that deals with the realities of your mutual situation. If you simply go through a contracting process as if he were a willing client and you were an eager helper, the lack of discussion about the real situation will usually come back to haunt you later in the project. In such situations, I have acknowledged captive clients, and I have best served them by figuring out how to disengage from the project gracefully and still save face with the boss. Clients have felt that this was a real service, and far more useful than going through ritual motions.)

To aid in the preliminary stages with a new client, I have developed a simple checklist (Figure 2.2) with questions I want to be sure to ask myself about the potential project, the clients, and the issues that are likely to affect the success of my efforts.

Middle Phase

The middle phase of a project has the meat of the content in it: diagnosing, planning, and doing the work. As

Figure 2.2. Starting Issues: A Checklist

The following are some questions that can be asked when one is beginning a relationship as a consultant or provider of some help or service. Some of these questions will be ones you already use, some may expand on current questions, and some may suggest new areas to clarify.

1. Who initiated the contact and how?
2. What is the history of dealing with this problem area?
3. What does this tell me about potential sources of energy, motivation, and resistance to change?
4. Why is the client involved? Why am I?
5. Who is the client?
6. Am I connected at the right points in the system to be effective?
7. What are all the kinds of things that I know about the situation (including informal knowledge that I might not consider to be relevant because it wasn't labeled "data")?
8. What are the outside or environmental forces that control or constrain how much the client can change or use my help? Can these forces be influenced?
9. What is the preliminary definition of the task, or problem, or goals for the project? What are my needs and those of the clients?
10. Is this a situation where I can contribute effectively? What am I providing and what skills do I need? Am I an appropriate resource for the client?
11. Is this a situation where I should use my energy; is it an appropriate project for me?
12. What other resources might be needed by the client and can I help obtain them?
13. Where does my activity fit into the larger pattern of the client's work processes? How crucial is this effort, what else can it affect, what will affect it?
14. What are we contracting about, and how formal should it be?
15. With whom should the contract be developed?
16. What is our time frame? How long should the starting phase be in terms of running time or amount of work?
17. Have we shared our expectations concerning what we each expect to get from and give to the other?

18. Have we built-in a relatively natural means for renegotiating the contract, as well as a process for signaling that we feel renegotiation is needed?

19. Have we included areas in which each of us has influence, and are there enough for each of us to feel powerful?

20. How will we evaluate if the project is effective and do any necessary follow-up?

21. Have I negotiated with the client that I will be able to use the data from this experience when dealing with other present or potential receivers of my services? With what stipulations on the client's part?

---

mentioned before, diagnosis should include both the technical aspects of the problem area and the issues which are likely to arise during the working process. Most of us who have had experience with different kinds of clients and situations can sense early on the working difficulties we will have, but we tend to ignore these intuitions. In fact, they are relevant to a key part of our professionalism; *how* we do what we do. Recording such hunches and keeping track of them will help in diagnosing process problems before they become crises.

During the discussion of the Kolb-Frohman model, we noted that planning the actual steps in the project is generally most helpful if it is done in conjunction with the client. The same is true for reviews and on-going tracking of your progress. If you can define this stage as a joint concern, your service has less the air of a magician pulling rabbits out of hats, and more that of a collaborative learning experience in which the client gets more than just an end product.

You should be prepared to raise the question about role expectations whenever you think they are awry. The client is less likely to do it, since he or she is usually worrying about many other responsibilities and roles besides being your client. It should be one of the consultant's primary concerns, as it reflects a professional approach to both technical knowledge and the skills that apply that knowledge and guide clients.

Ending Phase

Finishing a project well is as important as starting it well, especially since the end is often what is remembered and transmitted to others. Endings are typically not handled very well in our society. We avoid them, don't talk about our mixed feelings, and tend to drift rather than make conscious choices. This is just as true for internal consulting projects; there is a definite lack of crispness. However, this lack of clarity is particularly costly to an internal consultant since he remains in the system and can be looked to for continual help whether or not there is an actual contract. This pattern results in a net energy drain on everyone unless a contract has been consciously renegotiated and a role of providing periodic, on-call support is defined for the consultant. This is an important consideration for staff *groups,* as well, since in the aggregate they can spend a good percentage of their time unproductively servicing old clients. Continuing, in this fashion, out of guilt, duty, or altruism doesn't help the staff group or the clients, who consequently are not compelled to cope with the issues by themselves.

Any effective ending must include a competent and useful evaluation. Having pre-designed an evaluation, the test is to follow through with it. In busy staff groups it is always tempting to shortchange the evaluation so as to get on to the next action project (and because, in evaluation, one always runs the risk of not looking perfect).

It is worth fighting that tendency, though, because an effective evaluation process is part of how your image in the organization is built and maintained. If you leave evaluations to the client alone, then you leave the decision of what should be evaluated to the clients. This is obviously a mistake, since your professional view of performance should include both the client's needs and your own stan-

dards for both solving technical problems and personal performance. I suspect that both clients and consultants overplay the product and underplay the evaluation, so that   ✓
neither learns very much about how to do it better next time.

Summary

To sum up, the process flow makes a big difference to the feel of a particular project. You should try to shape it consciously so that it has good starting, middle, and ending phases, with each phase setting the stage for what follows. If you have a model in your mind of good process, you can consciously choose when and where you do things. You also have a basis for structuring events with clients and can help them understand why you want to do something a certain way. This is not meant to imply that you don't already have good ideas. Rather, the focus here, and in the rest of the book, will be on using awareness of role expectations and shaping as one basis for managing the different phases of a project. The point is to encourage internal consultants to be as knowledgeable about their roles, and how to manage them, as they are about their areas of expertise.

NOTES FOR CHAPTER 2

1. David Kolb and Alan Frohman, "An Organization Development Approach to Consulting," *Sloan Management Review* Volume 12, No. 1 (Fall 1970), pp. 51–66. The description of the seven stages is a paraphrase of the original article.

What You Influence (The Organization as a Human System)

Understanding the characteristics of the organization in which we work may seem like an obvious and easy thing to do, but most organizational members in American society receive little or no explicit training to do so. What we do, instead, is to develop a blend of basic psychology and sociology courses, general systems theory, and folklore ("the ropes"), which we learn from more senior members. This folklore, however, is usually dependent on someone's specific experiences so that the "lessons" don't say much about the general characteristics of human systems.

Recently people have been studying human systems in a more formal way. This allows us to be more professional in our diagnoses and in understanding the human organization. The main idea in this chapter is that we are always potentially affecting aspects of the organization when we do our work, even though our roles may be defined only in terms of our technical specialties. We must accept as fact that our efforts may help a system to function more flexibly or more rigidly, accelerate reactions or slow them down, clarify work relationships or make them more fuzzy. We need to learn when we do these things, and how. This insight will allow us to make conscious choices not only about which projects to do but also about how to behave to have the maximum of desired results.

Characteristics of Human Systems

There are some basic aspects of human systems that are shared with other systems, such as biological systems. Both are made up of parts; these parts have relationships and transactions with each other; the parts have boundaries (rigid or flexible) that separate them from each other; the organization as a whole has a boundary separating it from its environment; it has transactions with the environment, giving and getting commodities such as information, materials, products, money, and people.

Still, this description does not tell us anything about a healthy human system. Barry Oshry and Karen Ellis Oshry, writing on organic social systems, provide an extremely useful basis for our practical understanding.

> All organic entities—individuals, groups, and systems—can be described in terms of the degree to which they are differentiated, generalized, integrated, and adaptive. The health or power of an entity is determined by its success in managing these processes. A healthy or powerful organic entity, one which is capable of surviving and developing in its environment, is one which is *differentiated, generalized, integrated,* and *adaptive.* Such an organic entity, whether an individual, a group or a total system, can develop a variety of specialized patterns of response to its environment (differentiation); despite this specialization among parts, each part to some degree maintains the capacity to serve the functions performed by other parts (generalization); all of these various parts can be mobilized into concerted action of the whole (integration); and the entity—individual, group, or system—can, in response to changing conditions in its environment, change its form, re-differentiate, change its pattern of integration (adaptability).
>
> Such an entity functions as a whole; it can interact complexly with its environment; the whole is not overly dependent on any of its parts; the parts, although performing separate functions, can function independently or in concert with one another; and the whole is capable of rearranging its parts and the relationships among these parts in order to respond more effectively to its environment and in order to cope with changing environmental conditions.[1]

When thinking of a human system such as a group in an organization, this definition of health also suggests ways in which a group can be "unhealthy":

1. A group may be under-differentiated. It may have the potential for developing a variety of response capabilities, but these possibilities are not realized.

2. A group may be un-integrated. It may have a variety of well-developed response capabilities, but is unable to mobilize these in concerted action.

3. A group may be under-generalized such that parts are overly dependent on one another, and if one or more parts are lost, the group can no longer function.

4. The group may be sclerotic such that it is unable to change its configuration when its current configuration is no longer adaptive or when a different configuration may be more adaptive.[2]

This way of thinking about system health, then, can be applied to an organization as a whole or to certain groups within it. However, the same basic issue arises at different levels: how well can the entity manage the processes of differentiation, generalization, integration, and adaptation?[3] Therefore, one way of defining an internal consultant's power would be to assess his ability to affect these four dimensions. To have power is to make a difference, and to have positive power is to influence differentiation, generalization, integration, or adaptability. Of course, these processes must be kept in balance and be appropriate for the demands of the surrounding environment.

Commodities to Work With

Barry Oshry's formulation of specific sources of system power is a useful means of seeing with what elements you can work to improve system health. These targets of influence cut across whatever the internal consultant's specialty area may be; there are inherent factors that exist in all social systems and are therefore potentially influenced by what you do, no matter how your area of specialization is defined. Oshry's theory is that we can mobilize or energize people in a system toward greater differentiation, or integration, for example, by conscious control of resources, structures, and boundaries (a detailed discussion of which follows).

Controlling Resources

Whenever we control commodities that other people value and want to obtain, we have the potential to energize others and ourselves by how we choose to use these resources. The resources can be *anything* that someone else values: information, ideas, money, personal time, commitment, food, recognition, personal esteem or regard. Sometimes we may *give* them money, favors, suggestions, and they respond productively by doing something that needs to be done. Sometimes we can energize ourselves and others by *denying* others resources that they want or need. By choosing not to give, we may also stimulate others to take action. We may also choose to use *tensioning* with resources, which is neither to give resources nor to rule out the possibility of giving them, but rather to say, "It depends, maybe I will, if...." We put a tension into the relationship which can be seen as a positive force if people act on it.

One point to remember is that giving, denying, or tensioning are not good things to do in and of themselves. It is a diagnostic question as to which action will be most helpful from the viewpoint of system health. The person in an internal consulting role has a built-in handicap in using tension, since the role is often defined as a "giving" one. Being committed to functioning as good "helpers," we believe the essence of our job is to give to those who want. But the fact is that in some situations we would contribute more if we were not so quick to give and considered all these responses as legitimate.

We tend to think in fairly narrow terms about what resources we can control. Staff people generally regard themselves as having less power as compared with line managers and top executives. But this feeling is based on the assumption that only certain high visibility commodities count: budgets, hiring decisions, job assignments. Consultants actually have a wide repertoire of not-so-visible commodities that others *may* care about: ideas, time, cooperation, recognition or friendship from the consultant, future support. We have to do some careful analysis to spot the more subtle requests and expectations which give us clues as to what our clients, colleagues, and bosses really care about.

Controlling Structures

Structuring is a process which occurs all the time in organizations, and it is a powerful means for shaping human activity and channeling energy. Structuring means creating the framework or settings within which human action occurs. Again the most obvious and conventional view of structuring is that it is done by creating reporting arrangements, with the organization chart as the way of representing such structuring. But there are many other kinds of structuring that occur throughout the life of an organization which influence its members' assumptions, expectations, and perceived constraints. Ongoing structuring means calling meetings, setting agendas, defining procedure, setting policies, deciding on physical structures, layouts, and locations of people and groups, writing job descriptions, setting goals for yourself and others, setting time deadlines, and creating procedures for follow-up and evaluation.

Sometimes the necessary energizing move is to *create or maintain* structures within which we function. If we do this well, if the forms we establish are appropriate, and if we maintain them sensitively over time, then we make possible the necessary interactions for a system's health. On the other hand, sometimes we can energize a situation by *abandoning* the structures which we have carried with us into a situation. We let go of the hope that the structures are "right," and we accept the evidence that they were either not appropriate or have outlived their usefulness. We allow new structures to fit the process, rather than trying to make all our processes fit the structures. And sometimes we create energy or movement by *tensioning*. That is, we act so as to call into question whether or not to hold on to a structure; and we push for getting more information in order to make the best choice.

The point here is again that internal consultants often take too limited a view of what they have to work with in controlling structures. Just because they do not have authority over their client's (or their own) organization charts does not mean that there are no ways in which they influence structures. The real question is whether or not the cumulative impact of various structuring decisions adds up to organizational health, or adds up to a net zero of random choices.

Controlling Boundaries

Much of the sense of identity of an organism comes as a result of boundary management: sharpening or reducing the separations between individuals, groups, and organizations. Controlling boundaries is therefore a potent means to influencing the events in an organization. We may energize a situation by opening up or loosening our boundaries. We open ourselves to information from the outside, we share more information with others, and we locate our activities in visible, accessible spots rather than in hidden, private locations. We become more informed and are able to interact with greater meaning with the people around us.

In other cases, we may close or tighten the boundaries. We stop the flow of information and demands, we stop being available and at the service of others, we make more selective choices, and we may also move our office to a less accessible spot.

There is no consistently "right" move in boundary management. The system may be having trouble because different groups get in each other's way. In this case, boundaries must be clarified and tightened. There may be too little information or resource sharing between units, so that they make bad decisions based on misperceptions. In this case, the boundaries need to be relaxed so that communication flow can improve. As we will discuss in the next chapter, one of the most important means to understanding system power is to judge when the client should be encouraged to pull away and develop his own power.

Implications for Consultant Activities

A consultant's behavior, on a day-to-day basis, is taken automatically by clients. And individual acts may seem trivial and inconsequential. Yet, at the same time, they can also intervene in the functioning of a human system. If chosen well, mundane actions can be moves toward improving system health even as they contribute to the technical problem area. The following examples represent only some of the possibilities.

Meetings: A consultant has many occasions to call meetings: to facilitate planning a project, to gather information about a client's problems, to share information. The choices about who to invite, where and when to hold the meeting, are structuring choices and can affect the subsequent structures of a client system. You may call together people from different units who have never been in the same room before. Although it was not the purpose of the meeting, the biggest effect of this temporary structure may be for the participants to leave with a recognition that they share interests and problems, thereby loosening the boundary between them. Conversely, you might decide to hold separate meetings with the two units and thereby reinforce the tight boundary between them.

Reports: Preparing and delivering reports is one of the most frequent tasks of the typical internal consultant, yet many of the systemic effects of how this is done tend to be unrecognized. Such choices as whether to do a report, when to do it, what to include, and who to share it with all can have system implications. For example, sharing your findings simultaneously with people at several levels of the client system creates a different kind of structure than presenting it only to the top person. The shared information can generate more energy for implementation and follow-up than having just one person hold all the results. In other instances, your contact with the client system may lead you to question whether you should do a report at all. Withholding a resource can energize the client to examine what he does with crucial information and whether it should so continue. (This will only happen, however, if you can articulate why you question the value of a report.)

Requests to Clients: The kinds of requests and expectations you communicate to your clients can serve two purposes: to get you what you need to perform your role as a helper and/or to change the structure of activities for the client system. Asking for a certain type of data regarding, say, the frequency of problems, can stimulate a new awareness of that problem as well as a new structure for putting it in the system. Sometimes seeing an old problem in a new context is all that is necessary to effect a change.

Location for Events: You can affect both boundary management and the distribution of scarce resources by *where* you choose to hold meetings or presentations. For instance, holding project briefings in a company's "Board

Room" breaks the norm if that room was characteristically used exclusively by the board of directors, as does meeting in different groups' conference spaces. That way team members can learn about groups that they knew very little about and had never felt comfortable visiting. It helps to be somewhat experimental about locations, as being locked into only one location wastes the opportunity to influence system characteristics.

Direct Suggestions: Another avenue for affecting system health is making direct suggestions about factors that you have sensed inhibit the effect of the client system. If the boundary between two groups is so tight that they are unlikely to support one another in implementing your solutions, then a discussion of boundaries can be included in your recommendations. If the structure of the client system is such that the people who know the most have no forum for expressing their views to people in power, then you can make a case for altering this structure. In each example, your own input about systemic features can be quite forceful if you base it on both (a) the fact that you need a different structure or boundary in order to be most effective in sharing your professional skills, and (b) the fact that the particular condition is blocking the client system from developing further competence (that would decrease the need for outside help).

The examples used here are meant to illustrate opportunities to get double mileage out of things that you would be doing anyway. The same implications can be drawn from activities such as choosing projects, making distribution lists for your announcements or summaries, writing memos, creating training and educational events, raising questions, or making telephone calls.

The primary point here is to stimulate consideration of several questions. What is a healthy human system, and how can I tell what a system needs at a particular time in order to become more effective? What am I doing that can both accomplish specific project goals and contribute to the health of the system? How much do I want to take responsibility for the impact of my actions on the organization and its members? The answers are obviously up to you to decide. In some cases it may be too complicated or inappropriate to do much active influencing of the client system itself (for example, when you have been hired for a strictly limited role on a specialized need or problem); in others you may find that without doing some influencing of the client system itself, your efforts will be wasted. Whatever the situation, I believe that we are ahead of the game if we are at least aware that this range of possibilities exists, and if we can take responsibility for both our own product and, to some degree, for the impact of our product and process on the client system.

NOTES FOR CHAPTER 3

1. Barry Oshry and Karen Ellis Oshry, "Middle Group Dynamics: Ramifications for the OD Unit," in W. Burke and L. Goodstein (eds.) *Trends and Issues in OD: Current Theory and Practice* (San Diego, California: University Associates, 1980), pp. 51–52.

2. Ibid., pp. 15–16.

3. This section is quoted or paraphrased from Barry Oshry, "Organic Power," (Boston, Massachusetts: PST, Inc., 1976). I am indebted to the Oshrys not only for their materials, but also for the many learning and work opportunities we've shared.

What Influences You?
(The System
as Context)

Understanding system dynamics is useful to internal consultants for two reasons: because they act in ways which *influence* that system, and because they are members of the system which provides the *context* in which they function. We now turn to the second of these, to examine the ways in which organizations help or constrain a consultant. Still, we must remember organizations are made up of people.

Positional Experiences

One fundamental point is that we see and experience the world from a particular vantage point. We have "positional experiences" that are not similar to those of someone who is in a different position. This may seem like an obvious assumption and yet we often behave as if it were not the case. We attribute someone's actions entirely to personality ("That's the kind of person Jack is...") and think that merely getting a different type of person into a position will solve recurring problems. The view of experiences as positionally determined suggests that someone is behaving differently than we think we would because his location in the system leads him to perceive and experience it differently. He has different opportunities to hear about new developments, or different contacts, or different time restrictions. All of these factors lead to varying pictures of the organization and one's position in it.

This is one of the hardest things to remember as we go about our work. Although we each think that we are "reality centered" and see the world accurately, our positions in the system help shape our views and, as a result, the world can look very different. Two people can be equally reality centered and still be dealing with separate realities. It becomes very difficult to communicate, especially if the two people assume that they are responding to the same image, and this assumption is not tested.

One of the interesting distinctions that Barry Oshry has made is the difference in experience and perception among the top, middle, and bottom levels of an organization.[1] Each of these strata has its own image of the system, the crucial system problems that need attention, the significant issues for members of that stratum, and the nature of members on the other levels. The top level members see certain patterns and issues that cut across the various subunits, plus they are usually in a position to perceive both demands and opportunities from the environment. Their responsibilities include such issues as how much to control and maintain structures, procedures, or directions. Middle level people see the world of the organization as if they were the meat in a bologna sandwich; they are pressed from the top by role expectations and pressed from the bottom because they are responsible for poor work conditions. Their dominant view of issues concerns how to simultaneously satisfy conflicting demands. Members of the lower level see where the actual work gets done and they get a less filtered view of what really happens in that process. What they don't get to see is the larger pattern and the pressure on the top members from outside the organization. The issues which bottom members face are how much to go along, fight against, or just get away from the demands and expectations of the system.

There are other positional dimensions that produce different viewpoints. Specialists tend to see the world differently than generalists and line managers; headquarters people work with a different image of the system in their heads than do field people; those who only deal with other units internal to the system have a different experience than members of buffer units that have regular contact with customers, suppliers, or government representatives.

The key point is that there is no single "right" view. Each position has advantages and disadvantages. There are always things to learn from other viewpoints, particularly as a means to a more differentiated, accurate view of what's influencing what in the organization.

The hardest time to remember this is when we apply it to ourselves in consulting roles. Although the concept of multiple views of reality may be well-known, it's very hard in practice to really *believe* that we may be distorting or selectively perceiving. What we see is what's there, or at least that's the way it feels. Whereas, the fact is that the usual internal consulting positions have obvious built-in limitations insofar as perceiving the system is concerned. Consultants often are not subject to the same mixture of demands, constraints, and reward structures which affect the client, so a consultant tends to be less aware of them. ("Too theoretical" or "blue-sky" is the way clients refer to this gap.) However, because the consultant works with different clients, he can see patterns that are not readily visible to a client. Occasionally, the client is very important in the organization and therefore concerned about "top-type" issues, while the consultant is without a level, working with several different strata. This tends either to make the consultant very sensitive to such concerns *or* to make him unaware of this fundamental difference, since the consultant does not experience the pressures of the system's hierarchy.

All that need be said here is that these differences in positional experience and viewpoint do exist. They are a fact of social system life, and consultants are not immune. We can do a better job of relating to clients and meeting their expectations by recognizing this fact and using it as a guide. The most important aspect is to be curious about the world-views of your client and colleagues. If you really want to know how they see the world and what it is about their positions that supports this view, you are unlikely to plow merrily ahead believing you are the only person who is truly reality centered.

Other System Forces

Besides positional experiences, there are other systemic forces—a mixture of structures, boundaries, and resource control patterns—which either constrain or enhance your ability to make things happen for your clients and the organization. The context in which an internal consultant works would presumably vary from one organization to another. So it is really a diagnostic question as to which forces are helping and which are hindering in your particular system. To demonstrate, however, the kinds of forces one might see, I'm including the results of one such study (Figures 4.1 and 4.2). Over one hundred members of a large organization were asked to list the system forces which either constrain or enhance their power to provide effective help.

This particular profile is not general to all organizations, but is illustrative of the context that such forces can create. In the case presented here, the responses were affected by a recent shift from a centralized total organization to a more decentralized group of sub-unit "companies," who were expected to obtain resources as best they could. The role of staff groups was also changed to include "selling" their services to clients who, previously, had been a captive market. These changes are reflected in the study's results.

As in most positions, internal consultants face pros and cons: they have a measure of security and freedom as members of the system and have been given support via employment. On the other hand, in addition to low status and little authority, they are stretched thin by conflicting demands on their time.

Figure 4.1. Forces which Increase Internal Consultant's Influence

---

From the Consultant:
- Not profit-oriented as a unit, competes with outside consultants
- Greater freedom to use professional personnel

From the Client:
- No expertise in our specialty in the sub-units
- Confusion among units over long-term directions
- Trend toward a younger population that is more comfortable using specialists (not threatened)

From the Corporate Social System:
- Increased governmental problems resulting from reorganization, compliance
- Move to decentralization, more freedom to seek out resources
- Risk-taking is encouraged
- Pushing responsibility and authority to lower levels
- Push in the system for change for change's sake
- Encouragement from corporate to increase our visibility
- Corporate has shifted accountability for tax compliance to sub-units

---

The attributes of a client group that tend to increase a consultant's influence are: confusion resulting from any reorganization, lack of specialized resources (but the need for them due to more autonomy), and some willingness to experiment due to the presence of a younger management. The forces which work against the consultant are: confusion, physical dispersion, power blocks, and a client's freedom to solicit external help.

The corporate system itself also affects a consultant: the change in structure has led to higher expectations of the sub-units, more complex governmental regulation problems with which these units must grapple, and the pressure for further change and experimentation. Conversely, the system's historic climate of paternalism has worked against

Figure 4.2. Forces which Decrease Internal Consultant's Influence

From the Consultant:
- Expertise spread thin because of demands
- Little or no participation in long-range planning
- Loss of functional authority; have to help rather than do
- Tend to have lower hierarchical status than client

From the Client:
- Units have option to use outside consultants so tend to overvalue them, undervalue us
- Dispersion of physical locations, (we're less visible and their problems are less visible to us)
- Reporting relationships can keep clients from making own decisions about using help
- Lack of client group planning, don't know when they need help

From the Corporate Social System:
- Priorities not set at top
- Lack of skills for specialized areas
- Job bidding system with a lot of movement among units, can't build stable helping relationship
- Tendency to use staff as scapegoats for system problems
- Lack of uniform operating procedures across sub-units
- Paternalism, doesn't pressure sub-units to do better, improve, change

steady improvement. The move toward decentralization seems to have reduced the sense of common performance standards for which to strive (and hence client's need for assistance in meeting these standards); and a fluid job bidding system has led to increased job mobility and the consequent loss of established relationships.

It is clear, then, that the environment for an internal consultant's efforts in this company is neither all good nor all bad. Readers might generate similar lists of the forces at work in their own systems and then consider how to com-

pensate for the negative factors and how to take greater
advantage of the positive ones. We will return to this subject
later when we compare external and internal consulting
roles.

System Impact on Consulting Group Power

The kinds of system forces here described also have pronounced influence on the power and effectiveness of those
in staff roles. As with client or consultant groups, there are
features which either help or hinder staff attempts to function as a team and help other units of the organization.

For instance, various management studies have indicated three broad characteristics of organizational units
that have the power to influence other groups. One is that
they have _non-substitutable resources_ (ideas, services, or
products) which they control and which other units need.
This is analogous to the resources control process already
discussed. And the converse also tends to be true: internal
units whose services and products can easily be obtained
elsewhere tend to be lower-power.

Second, powerful units tend to be _central_. That is,
they are in the middle of events, transactions, or information flow. They have the option to open or close the boundaries between other groups and themselves because they find
out what is happening in time to actually do something
about it. This centrality is a structural characteristic and can
refer both to physical centrality (being visible instead of in a
satellite office where no one ever visits) and social centrality
(the unit is on key information distribution lists, members
are included in high-level conferences). The process is somewhat circular, however, since it's hard to tell whether the
centrality leads to potency or the potency leads to centrality.

The third factor is _a unit's ability to reduce uncertainty for other units_. This could be by being able (and will-

ing) to structure events or situations, to make decisions and stand behind them, and to provide information to other groups who do not know what's happening in and outside the organization. Although staff groups will sometimes shrink from taking the risks involved, those that do take that action become important to the unit, as well as being a real force in the organization.

The more common situation is one where the staff consulting group tends to be relatively low-power and its members feel weaker than the line organizations and even than other staff units which are seen as "in favor" with top management. To illustrate the system dynamics that leads to this low-power stance, we will examine a case presented by the Oshrys in "Fear and Loathing in the Middle."[2]

The Oshrys use the example of the internal organization development (OD) unit whose mission is to promote healthy organizational structures, processes, and problem-solving throughout the system. In practice, they say, OD units have the following characteristics:

1. Members do not derive much personal nourishment from their direct association with the unit.

2. Members feel that the real action lies in the client groups they are servicing and not within their own unit.

3. Efforts at sharing joint problem-solving or consultation within the units often fall flat. Members tend to be disinterested in one another's projects . . . and resist being burdened by their colleagues' problems.

4. Unit interactions are often marked by a complex of unresolved interpersonal problems; members don't like one another and they have difficulty communicating and working with one another.

5. Members do not feel that the unit, regardless of the words used to describe it, is a team; it feels and acts like a collection of individual contributors.

6. Unit members place low priority in their own meetings. Meetings with clients take precedence and are often scheduled such that, for meetings of the OD unit, members arrive late, leave early, or don't come at all.

7. One or more unit members are scapegoated as the cause of low group commitment . . . yet the problem remains the same even as these members leave the unit and are replaced by others.

8. The unit fluctuates between working on becoming a group . . . versus giving up on becoming a group. . . . This latter feeling reflects the belief that whatever power exists in the OD unit comes from the actions of individual members and that there is no special power inherent in the unit as a whole.[3]

Their point is that these characteristics are not a function of being an OD unit, but are rooted in systemic experiences of *middle groups,* that is, units within a system which, by the nature of their intended functions, are expected to be responsive and of service to other units in the organization. "Middleness" is defined as being between the system's top and bottom levels, and therefore, being expected to provide help, support, and comfort to both. Middle groups are to be responsible and loyal to the hierarchy and also responsive to the needs of a variety of sub-units. The powerlessness, isolation from one another, lack of mutual interest and collaboration on each other's projects, and lack of commitment to the group can all be seen as consequences of the middle unit's position in the system.

Middle space is a diffusing space, which tends to pull people apart internally and from one another. It is a space which encourages continuous movement rather than stability; it is a tourist's space, mostly away and rarely at home; it is an outsider's space, interacting with people who are close with one another and separate from oneself; it is an other-directed space,

encouraging increased responsiveness to others and little concern for self....

The uncontrolled dynamics of Middleness draw Middles to a
condition of over-differentiation and low integration. The
Middle group, in response to its system dynamics, literally dis-
integrates. It is the diffusion of the Middle position which pulls
people apart internally and from one another, and, as that diffusion continues unrecognized and uncontrolled, the differences among members develop (differentiation), members
grow more isolated, more out of touch with one another (de-
creased generalization); and the group ceases to function as an
integrated whole.[4]

But the Oshrys also point out that diffusion and
powerlessness are not inevitable outcomes of middle group
space. A staff unit that recognizes and manages the pressures on itself can use middleness as an advantage:

Such a group reaches out to, interacts with and collects information about a variety of other units within the system. Its
diffusion provides the opportunity for widespread data gather-
ing. Information gathered by any one part of the group is fed
back to the group and becomes information of the whole. The
group develops its specialized skills and services; yet the specialized skills developed by one part are also available to all
other parts of the group. Depending on the conditions existing
in client units, the group might replace one set of specialized
skills with another, or it might bring a variety of specialized
skills to bear on a given client situation.[5]

How does this apply to your own working unit?
From a system forces point of view, internal staff groups
tend to be over-differentiated, over-specialized, under-
generalized, and non-integrated, but each of these can be
used as a positive dimension to work on as a group. Points
of commonality and agreement can be discussed and dis-
covered, so that members experience generalization as well
as differentiation. Regularly sharing experiences in client

systems can help build a common data base. Thinking of the
unit as a "we" can lead to adaptive uses of resources by
changing consultant assignments when the client needs a
change.

Perhaps the most important structure which a helping unit can create to enhance its own impact is to build
regular events between group members, rather than between
unit members and client groups. As noted, the diffusing
pressures of client demands usually lead the staff group to
give low priority to their own meetings; and yet they really
need to do the opposite if they are to develop an *integrated*
unit. Regular times should be set for goal setting, information sharing, restructuring, and strategy development; and
these times should be honored, not ignored when any conflicting opportunity or demand arises. Although this may
feel like shortchanging a particular client, not doing it un-
wittingly shortchanges the whole organization.

To summarize the main theme of this chapter, the
organization within which a consultant works is both a target for influence and a context for the consultant's opera-
tions. It behooves an internal consultant to work at understanding human systems as organisms with comprehensible,
observable patterns and processes of their own. It is often
tempting to react to others' behavior in the system as simply
a function of who they are; and yet this behavior is more
often a function of their position in the social space and the
forces acting on them. Seeing events or behavior as related
to structures helps to clarify what we are trying to do, as well
as our own experiences.

We can try to make it both a better world for others
and a better world in which to do our work. This thought
may seem like a platitude, but many internal staff groups in
American organizations treat the dynamics and climate of
the organization as a given, rather than thinking it part of
their job.

NOTES FOR CHAPTER 4

1. Barry Oshry, "Power and Position," (Boston, Massachusetts: PSI, Inc., 1977).
2. Barry Oshry and Karen Ellis Oshry, "Middle Group Dynamics: Ramifications for the OD Unit," in W. Burke and L. Goodstein (eds.) *Trends and Issues in OD: Current Theory and Practice* (San Diego, California: University Associates, 1980), pp. 41–61.
3. Ibid., pp. 41–42.
4. Ibid., pp. 56–57.
5. Ibid., pp. 57–58.

Problems in Role Synchronization

49

Before turning to the topics of role analysis and role-shaping, I want to set the stage by discussing a set of situations that anyone in an internal helping role ought to recognize and influence. I am referring to certain predictable role problems which consultant and client tend to create for one another, so that they seem to be driving each other slightly crazy. This pattern is usually the result of a helping relationship where, although they are not aware of it, the parties' work worlds are structured differently. This non-synchronization (literally, being out of step with each other) is especially likely to occur if the consultant and client do not openly discuss and manage their mutual role expectations.

Consultant Actions that Irritate Clients

Non-synchronization of Time Patterns

One of the most insidious irritations occurs when consultant and client operate on different time systems. This is demonstrated in a number of ways, such as having different definitions of what "short-term" and "long-term" mean. If the client is operating in a high-action, high-stress environment, short-term will mean the next few days or weeks, and long-term will be a few months ahead. The typical consultant, however, might be thinking of long-term planning as years into the future. This difference can lead to tugs and pulls in which the client feels pushed to allot time, energy, and attention to issues too distant and with no perceived relevance or payoff.

Another example of the disparity between client and consultant is a recurring difficulty in scheduling meetings. Usually the client expects the consultant to be able to schedule a meeting on one or two days' notice, while the consultant is working on a personal schedule which cannot accommodate that need. Occasionally the reverse occurs. In each case, however, the person with the shorter planning horizon tends to feel that the other lacks commitment and/or is avoiding the project. In fact, the underlying cause is simply structural: non-synchronized time patterns that will always be a stumbling block unless they can figure out a way to meet each others' time structures, if only temporarily.

Assuming Inappropriate Authority

Some of the worst situations in internal helping relationships have been caused by the consultant's attempt to assume inappropriate authority. Even if the consultant is acknowledged to be expert in his field, any attempt to teach by issuing instructions and orders can grind on the client. The client is still responsible for his own job performance, and so is likely to feel uncomfortable when a consultant tries to make decisions which the client will ultimately have to defend. The more a consultant expects a client to show obedience or deference, the wider this gap will become, until the client will reject even those ideas or programs which are perfect. Ways will be found to quickly remove the bothersome consultant. If the consultant plays power games by using some higher executive's authority to coerce the client, although a slower process, the results are similar. The consultant may gain initial compliance, but it will be superficial and the client will still find a way to waste his time or get him out.

Taking an Arrogant Stance

This problem stems from placing a very high value on your knowledge, ideas, and opinions while dismissing the client's ideas as obviously being in need of continual correction. Even though you may have a great deal of experience and expertise, this stance reflects short-sightedness and lacks synchronization, as well. One reason, similar to the result of assuming decision-making authority, is that it will stimulate a client to look for ways to reject what you do or suggest, simply out of resentment. The other reason is that most serious managers have a great deal of acquired wisdom about their own work worlds, of which you are not aware. If you don't recognize and acknowledge this wisdom, it may mean that you have not become sufficiently involved in the client's world to fully understand it.

There is another, more subtle form of arrogance in cases where the consultant has been called in by a high-level executive to work on a project with employees who are below that executive's level in the hierarchy. Consultants sometimes give undue attention to their special relationship with the boss by making frequent cryptic allusions to inside information to which the working clients are not privy, and which the consultant has no intention of sharing. Although the consultant may be behaving unintentionally, this process tends to generate fantasies about what's going on, why the consultant is "really" there, and what surprise moves the boss is about to make. It can also solidify the client's attitudes against the consultant, making the job more difficult. ("He's so smart and well-informed, let him find it out for himself....")

In general, then, arrogance toward the client's views is both costly (because it creates resistance to your own influence) and a mistake (based on a lack of curiosity and/or a belief that no one could possibly be as perspicacious as yourself). One way to reduce the pull toward arrogance is to arrange for someone who knows both the client system and your own area to occasionally observe you and provide a reflection of your attitude and posture towards the clients.

Over-deference toward Clients

An impartial observer, however, can also encourage another and opposite trap: placing so much weight on the client's opinions that you defer even when you should not. You do not raise issues that contradict the client's beliefs; do not confront a client even when you know he is taking a poor approach to a problem in your field of expertise; do not talk about differences between you and the client; and do not make propositions and suggestions that can be tested or evaluated. This can be very frustrating for your client, especially when they sense you have a lot more to offer. Rather than giving the client a secure feeling about your expertise, you create a vague sense of uneasiness which the client can well do without.

Remaining Too Abstract

A typical instance of non-synchronization with members of a client group is to express yourself in an abstract manner as they are trying to absorb tangible suggestions, guidance, or products. Staff people tend to see subtleties and nuances in their areas of expertise, so that they will often resist the client's search for quick solutions (which the consultant sees as too simplistic). In resisting the naive solution, however, the consultant fails to provide enough concrete information and the client will not feel any sense of accomplishment.

There are, fortunately, concrete methods that help to synchronize this situation: specific recommendations for action; a progress report that is free of technical jargon; a "problems and issues" paper that uses specific, everyday examples from the client's own experiences; a thought piece that generalizes client problems, but also suggests new ways of looking at these problems; an event, such as a work-shop, to plan a specific response to a certain problem. The point is that if you do something that the clients can react to (regardless of how), you are more likely to meet their need for involvement and progress. Reports or papers, if done well, become indispensable tools that are referred to by managers months after their first presentation. They obviously serve the client's need for concrete "things" with which to work. An example from my own field: I designed a set of proposed guidelines for effective executive team meetings, which provided a set of specific dimensions for members to use in testing their own group's effectiveness or proposing alternative guidelines.

This bit of homey advice may seem totally obvious to staff people who earn their living from tangible studies, reports, and products. But even so, there can be a tendency to keep a client in the dark while "magic" is worked. But by keeping clients in the picture and explaining things in simple terms, they can understand *how* you produced what you did.

Burrowing-In

Of all the types of non-synchronization, burrowing-in is probably the easiest to understand and to remedy. It occurs when the consultant comes to feel too cozy in his or her home office area and, therefore, spends less and less time in the territories of present and potential clients. The consultant thinks that a fine job is being done. Meanwhile, the client concludes that the staff member is aloof and uninterested in "real world problems."

The main force pushing one toward burrowing-in is the need for security and certainty. Going to one's office, where it's obviously legitimate to be, is more comfortable than wandering into the shops, to the factory floor, or into an office area where one has no place to alight. This is especially true once a feeling of social distance has begun to develop, because the consultant then feels unwelcome and nervous about casually seeing what's happening. The best antidote for this pattern is to set up a structure of periodic visits. This contact will reduce the feeling of distance, which, in turn, will make the consultant return and wander the next time. Without establishing this counter-pattern, the consultant has no way of knowing the client's present situation— he can only hope to. Developing a role definition for yourself which includes planned wandering in a client's home territory removes the necessity for this kind of guesswork.

Clients Irritating Consultants

Since it may sound as if internal consultants are always the culprits in cases of role non-synchronization, I should add that there are also abundant examples of client culpability. Clients can annoy consultants by doing things which are out of synchronization with the consultant's roles. I have asked internal consulting groups to describe the ways clients make life difficult for them. The examples fall into four broad categories: inappropriate expectations, not meeting consultants' expectations, setting poor conditions for the project, and exploiting the consultants' internal status.

Inappropriate Expectations for the Consultants' Roles

Clients are irritating when they:

- Expect the impossible;
- Decide how we should do our work before there has been any real contracting;
- Want answers immediately, before any investigation;
- Negotiate a contract with our boss, then blame us for not meeting expectations that we don't know about and didn't agree to;

- Change expectations or groundrules unilaterally when we're halfway through a project.

It is easy to see how these kinds of mismatches can occur, especially if the consultant's world is relatively unknown to the clients, who don't have an instinctive feel for the work.

Clients Not Meeting Consultant Expectations

A number of the irritants stem from clients who are not doing enough, clients who:

- Can't or won't articulate their concerns;
- Don't use us as resources when they should (they involve us too late or not at all);
- Don't do the work that they are supposed to do to support our efforts;
- Put things off until there's a real crisis;
- Are disorganized about their own decision-making, so we can't get any momentum for implementation.

Creating Poor Conditions for the Project

Several examples are concerned with the setting or environment in which the consultant is to work. Again, these are instances where the clients' actions or style make it hard to do a good job, thereby increasing frustrations beyond the actual technical problems. The clients:

- Don't define what "it" is, yet blame us when we don't produce "it";
- Put limitations on our freedom of access or movement within their group, yet expect us to keep up with relevant facts and events;
- Provide us with inaccurate or too little information;
- Treat certain information as confidential, yet expect us to take it into account; they also spread information that we have been told not to spread.

Exploitation of the Consultant's "Insider" Position

Although it may seem like too strong a sentiment, consultants feel that clients sometimes exploit the fact that they are all members of the same larger organization rather than being independent of one another. The misuse (as felt by the consultants) of this connection occurs in a number of ways:

- Being used as an organizational "wedge" or tool in some power game between the clients and other groups in the system;
- Distorting client priorities or urgencies so that higher levels of the parent organization put pressure on the consultant to help them;
- Drawing consultants into ethical "gray areas" which don't fit our practices, but where we'd be disloyal if we blew the whistle on them;
- Getting elaborate proposals and costs estimates from us, then using these as the basis for hiring an outside contractor;
- Rejecting our help in favor of an outside consultant, then expecting us to help or train the consultants who have replaced us;
- Involving us in a risky project so we'll be the easily available scapegoat if it doesn't work out.

These exploitative maneuvers make consultants feel caught between the expectations of their own professional roles, on one hand, and the demands of the clients and the wider organization on the other. Actually, all four areas of irritation can feel like a squeeze if the consultant's attempts to provide a high-quality service are frustrated.

If we combine the consultant who annoys a client and clients doing the same to internal consultants, the pattern of non-synchronization seems reasonably clear. First, clients often see internally-based staff consultants/helpers as not being helpful or specific enough, while the clients see themselves as goal oriented, reality centered, and trying to do a job in a practical, no-nonsense manner. Conversely, internal consultants tend to see clients as having inappropriate expectations for the consultants' roles while at the same time failing to meet the consultants' needs for collaborative support, and not assuming responsibility.

When these pictures are baldly presented, it is obvious that both consultant and client overplay their good intentions and underplay those of the other party. They treat the experience of non-synchronization as a result of the other person's style and intentions. Rather, it should be seen as a natural outcome of living in different worlds of knowledge, having different positional expectations placed on them, and being subject to different paces and time pressures. In this view, non-synchronization occurs mainly because of structural causes which are built into the situation rather than particular personalities. (To test this, observe how the complaints tend to be reversed when the client becomes a consultant, and the consultant is the client.)

To say that non-synchronization is natural doesn't mean that it is inevitable and unchangeable. The purpose of this chapter has been to describe non-synchronization, not to show how to reduce it. But much of the remainder of this book is designed, in one way or another, to help readers reduce non-synchronization. These approaches will help in reducing the frequency or degree of non-synchronization in consultant-client role relationships. The first and most important step is recognition of both problem and cause. Feeling guilty about not meeting expectations is no way to test whether they are relevant and useful; you must step away and see those expectations as malleable.

Role Concepts
and Consultant
Role-Shaping

In order to deal effectively with problems in role synchronization, we need to appreciate the many ways in which social roles influence our work behavior. To this end, I would like to review the basic concepts related to roles, so we will have a common understanding of the term. This precedes a description of one model for analyzing the roles possible for an internal consultant: choices about what kind of help to give to the client, and the consequences of opting for these definitions. Chapter 7 considers how to cope with some of the practical problems associated with role-shaping: role confusion, role conflict, and role ambiguity.

Basic Role Concepts

There is still some confusion when we talk about consultant *roles,* even though the concept of social role was clarified by social psychologists over twenty years ago.[1] In our common language experience, American culture still uses (as one meaning) "playing a role" to indicate behaving in a false manner, or to look like something you are not. A role, as it is used here, is nothing more or less than a *set of expectations* for what a person in a certain social position (father, industrial engineer, personnel representative, or software consultant) should or should not do in order to perform their duties well.

For example, the role of a person who is functioning as a technical consultant to an engineering design group may be defined by the client group as: raising questions about design assumptions and approaches, attending design review sessions, suggesting criteria for performance standards, and writing periodic reports which evaluate the efforts of the group and suggest means for improvement. In addition, the consultant may also believe part of her role is to advise the group's leader on technical or process matters, and to be supportive to anyone proposing novel solutions that might be quickly rejected by the rest of the group.

A role definition can cover a number of specific aspects of behavior or be more general, such as "help us to do our job better." From the example, we can also see that there are several different definitions of the same role: the consultant's expectations of herself, the client's expectations (and these may vary in a group), her consulting group colleagues' expectations, and her boss's image of her role (see Figure 6.1).

Because the role is defined by different people, the consultant may experience *role conflict,* where the various parties' expectations do not agree. She may have one view of her role, and everyone else may have another one; her clients may disagree among themselves as to what they need; the clients may agree with her, but the consultant's boss and peers have a different view of what "professional" help would be to the client group. In the next chapter we will consider the consequences of these conflicts, as well as what can be done to resolve or reduce the associated stress.

Finally, it's also an open question whether the role definition, even though perfectly consistent among the different parties, is appropriate. The consultant has to be concerned whether the client's needs match the helping role.

How does the client form expectations for the consultant? There are several contributing processes at work. It is likely that the client has had prior experiences with consultants or advisers which may have encouraged an image of what a "real" consultant is, even if this was, obviously, dependent on whatever this particular consultant did. In addition, clients usually have some specific ideas about what

Figure 6.1. Role Expectations

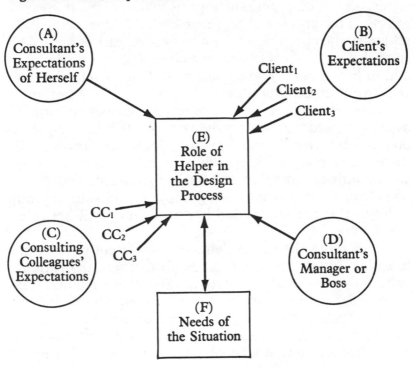

they want. The present consultant can help create the client's expectations by being explicit about her own view, and negotiating it openly with the client. This is an opportunity to shape a role based on the present client situation, rather than leaving it to the client's past association.

Types of Consultant Role Choices

Given the fact that both client and consultant have expectations about the role the consultant should take in providing assistance, what dimensions can we use to be more aware of our choices as consultants? What are we choosing to do or not do, and what difference does it make?

One simple model describes three broad types of roles which an internal consultant can play with his clients: the expert, the resource, and the process consultant.[2] Although they will be described as separate options, they are not really meant to be "pure" types. The point is rather to highlight several dimensions of choice that one considers (intentionally or accidentally) in helping someone. In practice, you may do all of your work in one mode on a project, or begin in one and shift to another as the project progresses.

The Expert Role

When a consultant is working in the expert mode, he tends to be doing something for clients that they can't or choose not to do for themselves. Sometimes, this role is desirable because the client system doesn't have the specialized knowledge to solve certain problems or do certain tasks. The clients may also not have the time, so they have a consultant work as an "extra pair of hands." Expert consultants work on specific problems or tasks; they diagnose a problem, generate solutions, and predict the consequences of these actions.

What are familiar types of expert consultants? Information systems specialists often work in this mode, doing some specific system design project or solving specific system problems. Consulting engineers and industrial engineers do the same, with their focus being on a project or problem that the clients can't or won't do themselves. Some personnel specialists play this role on specific problems with line managers. Doctors often take this stance, assuming the authority and responsibility for their client's health; and lawyers often take responsibility for legal problems about which their clients are assumed to be relatively naive.

This expert consultant is most useful to a client when they are dealing with a new, unfamiliar problem; when the clients do not have the expertise, and won't need it often enough to make it worth developing for themselves; when there is a crisis or deadline which presses clients to seek the quickest possible solution; and when the commitment of other clients to the consultant's solution is not too crucial to the success of the solution.

Conversely, the expert mode is less appropriate when it is important that the clients feel real "ownership" in the solution; when there is not a clear definition of the problem area; when no early solution or product is likely; and when the clients do not want, over the long term, to be dependent on outside help.

The label, "expert role," does not mean that consultants who operate in the resource and process roles are *not* experts. All three may have great *expertise* but the emphasis here is on role *behavior,* or the stance toward the client and what is done with that expertise. The expert role accentuates the difference between what the consultant knows how to do and what the clients can do for themselves.

The Resource Role

In the resource role, consultants help the clients do some task or solve some problem, rather than doing it for them. Resource consultants are experienced people who can serve as sounding boards, raise new questions, generate new approaches to problems, provide information to help clients diagnose a problem or think of new solutions. The emphasis here is on helping the clients do a task or solve a problem, as opposed to the expert role where it is the consultant's responsibility.

Examples of consultants in the resource mode would be investment analysts, when the decisions still rest with the client, working boards of directors in relation to a company's top management, some computer and information system consultants, corporate health and safety specialists helping subsidiary companies, personnel specialists working with line managers, and management consultants who provide new points of view and information.

The resource role mode tends to be most useful when a problem area is well defined. For example, when the client needs concrete ideas in order to choose a solution, when the client is locked into certain solutions and needs new alternatives, and when the client feels competent to take action and use the information which the consultant provides. This role is less useful when the problem area is not clear, when the client system doesn't have the resources to use the consultant's ideas very well, when there is a crisis and an expert consultant is needed to do a job completely, and when a more fundamental process problem calls for a process consultant.

The Process Role

A consultant working in the process role focuses on the ways in which the client is tackling the problems, rather than on providing a solution. The process consultant helps the client to recognize, define, diagnose, and solve the problem independently. He may engage in questioning why certain approaches are being used, suggest the consequences of a particular action or non-action, do educational and training activities to expand the client's awareness and capabilities, or just watch what the client does, to understand better his way of working.

Some organization development specialists tend to play this role, as do certain kinds of therapists, some personnel and human resource specialists, and systems specialists. This mode is most useful when the client is willing to assume primary responsibility, when the problems are complex and not well-defined, when there is a need for strong client group commitment to problem solutions and courses of action, and when there will be a continuing need for problem-solving skills in a particular area. The process role is not appropriate when the clients don't want it, when there is a need for specialized expertise which does not exist in the client system, and when there is a crisis situation which the client wants the consultant to resolve as quickly and as well as possible, regardless of any possible learning experience.

To clarify the differences between the expert, resource, and process modes, let's take a simple example. The manager of a large machine shop in an industrial products manufacturing company calls an internal corporate consultant to talk about whether the consultant can help solve a recurring problem with "housekeeping." The shop tends to be continually dirty, and scrap materials present a safety hazard.

In the expert mode, a consultant would take responsibility for diagnosing and solving this problem, with the client providing information. In the resource mode, the consultant would also seek information, but would focus on helping the clients to diagnose and solve the problem, while providing questions, suggestions, information about what others have tried, and alternatives that have not been considered. In the process role, the consultant would seek information, but the emphasis would be on *how* the clients have been working on the problem. The consultant's goal would be to improve the client's process for dealing with the housekeeping and other similar problems.

When they are matched with one another, the client is implicitly asking the expert consultant, "Can I rely on you to solve my problem or do a job for me?" He is asking the resource consultant, "Can you help us solve our problem or do our task? Do you add something that we don't have in the way of skills, information, or approach?" The client asks the process consultant, "Can you help us change the processes we use in working and solving problems, so that we do this better in the future?"

Since a role is a set of expectations, Figure 6.2 summarizes the key expectations associated with the three role types. The expert role tends to carry expectations of short-term, concrete results with the responsibility for success and

Figure 6.2. Expectations for Different Types of Consultant Roles

Area of Expectation	Role Type		
	Expert	*Resource*	*Process*
Responsibility for Products or Changes	Consultant	Combined	Clients
Amount of Content Input by Consultant	High	Medium or Variable	Low
Time or Commitment Required of Clients	Low	Medium	High
Short-term, Visible Change in Output or Products	High	Medium	Low
Amount of Change in Clients' Capabilities	Low	Medium	High

commitment of time and energy being primarily with the consultant. The resource role tends to be mixed, with shared responsibility and a mixed output of resource or process mode; but only expert, resource, and process modes require increasing amounts of self-exposure by the clients, in that order. The expert mode is thus an easier place to start unless the clients are already willing to commit themselves to self-examination.

There is also no "right" role for a consultant; it depends on the client's needs, the problem situation, and the stage in the process. Choosing a role is a diagnostic question, not a moral or an absolute one. What is important is that there be role synchronization: a good match between the role you assume and the expectations and desires of the client. For instance, some of the most frustrating moments have undoubtedly been when the client wanted someone to play the expert role and the consultant behaved in a process mode with a long time frame and heavy expectations for the client's involvement. Part of an internal consultant's professional functioning, then, should be to be aware of the expert/resource/process choice; to clearly negotiate expectations with the client early in the project; also to establish the fact that the appropriate consultant mode might change at a later stage; and to negotiate such changes in expectations when they become relevant (such as when you have produced a report, but realize that the key issue now has become what the client system *does* with such reports). It is important to remember that when you try to change your own role, you also put pressure for change on the client's role, since they are reciprocal. Shifting unilaterally generally leads the client to feel that you are not meeting expectations and have somehow violated the contract, even if he is not exactly clear about what is different or why it should matter.

On the other hand, it's just as important not to be locked into performing in only one mode. Consultants can trap themselves into doing what makes them feel comfortable rather than what the client needs. In the long run, especially for internal consultants whose reputations are quickly transmitted throughout the organization, this will only stereotype you as a "one-issue" or one-mode consultant. If you can operate with some flexibility and in a manner which keeps the issue of role expectations negotiable, then you will be more likely to be seen as a relevant resource for a variety of client needs.

Sharing the *process* of making role choices with a client is a means to having the client feel some joint responsibility for how the project goes. It also helps the client to see role shaping not as a mysterious process, but as a natural part of managing a relationship in a goal-oriented and responsible manner. One way of sharing these choices is to explain the expert/resource/process model to the client so that you have a common language for identifying and agreeing about the kind of help each of you wants to give and receive. Of course this simple model is by no means the only way to establish such a common language. Any role descriptions that provide a sharp picture of what is appropriate would be useful. Common societal roles, such as doctor, lawyer, policeman, teacher, or electrician, can be used as metaphors when discussing roles, provided that you use them as just a starting point. It would still be necessary to go beyond the labels and identify what behaviors are suggested. The goal is not to have elegant, "right" definitions of your reciprocal roles, but to agree on definitions and how they relate to each other.

NOTES FOR CHAPTER 6

1. For a classic compilation of role concepts, see Bruce Biddle and Edwin Thomas (eds.) *Role Theory: Concepts and Research* (New York: John Wiley and Sons, 1966).
2. I would like to acknowledge the origin of this model, but its history is hard to determine accurately. Similar versions have been summarized by Edgar Schein in *Process Consultation in Organization Development* (Reading, Massachusetts: Addison-Wesley, 1969) and by Gordon and Ronald Lippitt in "Multiple Roles of The Consultant," *The Consulting Process in Action* (La Jolla, California: University Associates, Inc., 1978), pp. 27–44.

Coping with Consultant Role Ambiguity

No matter how well specific projects are discussed and defined with a client, certain aspects of the internal consulting role still create an ambiguous situation. First, you're often working in areas that are not predictable or clear-cut; if this were so, the clients would probably have done the work themselves. But much of this unpredictability seems to go with the nature of the position you are in, not the content of the work itself. This chapter will describe some of the main causes of consultant role ambiguity; examine some of the consequences of consistent ambiguity for the consultant, the client, and the organization of which they are members; and suggest some strategies for effectively coping with ambiguity.

Causes of Internal Consultant Ambiguity

The sources of role ambiguity for internal consultants can be roughly grouped into four categories: what you do (structural ambiguity based on the position); how you do it (choices and options about modes of working); how you are evaluated; and what happens to you as a result (career path characteristics).

What You Do

There are a number of sources of ambiguity which are literally built into the job of many internal consultants.

They are not necessarily true for all consultants, or true all the time, but they form a definite pattern.

- The basic job description is often less definite, with fewer specifications and direct responsibilities, than for a line manager. More flexibility is needed in order to be responsive to a variety of client needs, and it is assumed that a professional will be able to structure his or her job responsibilities with only some general guidance.

- The temporary nature of task relationships leads to uncertainty about how long the project or relationship will and should last. Whether and when to end is always an implicit question while work is being done, as opposed to the more stable, regular pattern of most jobs.

- Even the process of defining projects may be somewhat loose so that the consultant may or may not be able to commit himself to a client without higher approval; and in many instances project definition is done collectively by consultant, client, and a consultant's manager.

- For central corporate service groups, there is a built-in tension over whether the consultant is simply providing help to a client in the sub-units of the organization or also acting as a central monitor/controller for excellence in an area of expertise and responsible to the company as a whole.

- The role of certain staff or consulting units is to deal with problems caused by environmental turbulence: as the outside world changes, consulting groups help line units to deal with these changes. Thus, the staff groups have to absorb the uncertainty that would otherwise cause problems for other units.

- Finally, the resources available to you may be more vague than in more direct line positions. What you have to work with may be flexible and become apparent by trying to use funds, information, or help from others, rather than having these limits already determined.

How You Do It

There are several sources of ambiguity which relate to the typical modes of working for internal consultants.

- The scope of decision-making authority is often only vague, and depends on the particular client situation and the consultant's willingness to take risks.

- The legitimate initiatives of the internal consultant are less confining than for line managers concerning such actions as: who you can contact, about what, at what levels; what events or meetings you can set up; what information you can seek, and from whom.

- There are "style" questions about how much the consultant should fit the norms of the organization for use of time, schedules, location for activities, rather than creating a more specialized pattern that fits the particular specialty area.

- There is also the requirement to choose among a number of action alternatives: you need to decide when to *help,* when to *encourage,* when to just *do* a piece of work, and when to *confront* the client with your judgment that what he wants you to do is not correct. All of these are "reasonable" actions, and the trick is diagnosing when to do which ones.

- Being an internal consultant, you must continually justify your existence, either because you charge your client directly or because he pays in overhead charges; the ambiguity comes in how to balance helping the client as he needs it as opposed to selling your services as you must.

How You Are Evaluated

Whether you continue to sell your services and get rewarded depends, in part, on how your work is evaluated. Internal consultants often experience considerable role ambiguity around the evaluation process.

- Goals for internal helpers are often written (if at all) in general terms, such as "to be responsive to requests for help from client groups," which don't allow for concrete measures of effectiveness.

- Besides the measures, the standards for high performance are often fuzzy compared with line positions, and may be based as much on how you look while working as on what you produce.

- Who *sets* the standards by which you are evaluated? This can be your boss, clients, professional colleagues, yourself, or some combination.

- There is often a large time delay between taking action and finding out what effect you had—if in fact you get any feedback at all. Sometimes you do, sometimes you don't.

- Staff units in organizations may be headed by general managers who are not professionals in that area, but are placed there to broaden their experience. As a result, they may have relatively little basis for evaluating the technical competence and performance of the group's members.

What Happens in the Long Run

The fourth area of ambiguity is in the career paths and opportunities available to the internal consultant: What will the future hold, and how can the consultant influence his or her future? Again, these questions tend to be much less clear than with more structured line management positions.

- The organization seldom provides a line of feedback to the staff group as a unit, nor is there very much opportunity for them to affect their career options from a total group stance.

- The typical career paths for line people are relatively clear and well-known in a system, while the opposite tends to be true for staff and consultants; their "advancement" in the organization is often a problem for both the organization's leadership and themselves. There is a truncated set of possibilities as long as advancement is defined as moving "up" in the organizational hierarchy.

- It is also not obvious that internal consultants will be considered relevant for other types of positions, even if they might in fact be well qualified; they become stereotyped as specialists and then forgotten.

- While line managers' careers in the organization are generally influenced by their individual performances (as evaluated by a higher manager), internal consultants' future possibilities may be controlled by policy decisions about whether or not to maintain a capability in their area of expertise. Their future may be non-existent, even when they have done an outstanding job up to the time of the decision to reduce or eliminate their specialty area.

Consequences of Role Ambiguity

If we assume, then, that internal consulting roles have features built into them which tend to generate role ambiguity, what effects does this ambiguity have on the consultants and the functioning of the organization? This naturally depends somewhat on the particular person, the situation, and the culture of the particular organization. There are, however, a few main effects which can be identified. You may also find new responses in the last section of this chapter.

One of the most common effects of prolonged consultant role ambiguity is the stress which leads to anxiety and doubts about one's ability. Other members' needling jabs, about seeing the consultant as "just an overhead burden, with no visible means of support except their paycheck," are taken to heart and the consultant can feel like a burden. The anxiety may be very generalized, with a continual feeling that things aren't right, even when the consultant can't point to any single element as being the cause of dissatisfaction.

A related effect is what we might call an "energy ooze," where the consultant is regularly putting in a significant amount of time, energy, and attention toward clarifying ambiguities in daily work life. This makes a big deal out of simple, automatic choices such as where and when to go to work on a given day, what to report about (as well as when to report, and to whom), and even how to dress. The cumulative effect is a lot of energy being taken up with the mechanics of doing rather than being focused on the content of the client's problems. If this effect is widespread among staff groups, the system tends to deal with special problems with relative inefficiency and at considerable expense.

If consultant role ambiguity is consistently too stressful for the comfort of the people who are expected to function in this mode, they will tend to leave consulting positions and shift into more defined, structural positions. The effect on the organization is consistent movement of people out of specialized helping roles into more traditional line positions, which may not be a good distribution of resources and skills if the system needs more flexibility in attacking problems. As is typical of such cases, the effect is even more costly because the most skilled people are the ones who will tend to leave a system first if they find it a poor climate for defining and supporting internal helping roles. On the average, these employees usually have the most opportunities to move to other organizations.

Although the emphasis here has thus far been on the costly effects of role ambiguity, there is a major area of potential benefit, as well. Ambiguity can provide unusual degrees of freedom for defining one's own style, pace, and pattern of work experiences, consequently providing a number of interesting payoffs to the consultant. Personal freedom is an obvious one; another is the room to maneuver within the organization's political processes, since legitimate influence actions are not explicit. The consultant also has an opportunity to shape the pattern of projects and challenges she takes on, thus managing her own areas of learning

and growth. Employees in more traditional positions tend
to learn relatively little about managing their own growth
process, since career decisions are made for them (and "for
their own good") by higher levels in the organization. By
contrast, there can be great opportunities in internal consultant positions for practicing and learning the process of
self-directed learning: what to work on, how challenging a
project should be in order to promote learning without it
being too threatening, how to balance action and thought so
that you learn from experiences, and how to structure situations so that you have some room for experimentation and
occasional failure without it being seen as a disaster for
your career.[1]

Coping with Role Ambiguity

The final question concerns options for dealing with role
ambiguity. From the previous discussion we can assume
that consulting roles inside an organization tend to have ambiguous aspects to them. We also know this ambiguity is
more pronounced in some organizations than in others, and
the consultant's actions also contribute to this situation.
What are some strategies that can be used to manage the
ambiguity rather than having it manage you? Some of these
approaches were implied in the role definition discussion
(Chapter 6), and new suggestions follow.

Role Negotiation

The most straightforward strategy is direct negotiation about role expectations. Negotiations need to be done
with clients, with colleagues, and with superiors in the hierarchy. The important issues concern style, how you will get
started in a project, goals for the client and for yourself, time
expectations, what you'll do with information, how new
projects can be identified, who can terminate a project, and
how it should be done. Such a discussion should also include

specific duties and quantitative constraints such as budget and hiring guidelines.

This role negotiation early in a project can be a great help in managing ambiguity if it sets an expectation about later *role renegotiation*. If you establish a norm in which either the client or consultant can propose further clarification or changes in expectations (for example, shifting from an expert into a process role mode), then ambiguity will only be a problem if you don't renegotiate.

Sharing Uncertainty

A similar strategy is to share the ambiguity problem with your client, your boss, or whoever is relevant. This move requires risking the embarrassment of not looking perfectly on top of everything in a project; but the alternative is always to hide the problem and thereby allow yourself and others to treat the unproductive uncertainty as your problem. For example, if your boss and a key client are placing mutually conflicting expectations on you, a high-leverage move would be to have a meeting where you disclose to them exactly what's going on and work on alternatives for improvement. The point is to try to get them to "own" the problem that the three of you share. It is not just your problem to be "competent" or good enough to meet both sets of demands. Many of those situations are sucker games where you can't satisfy both expectations, and the sooner you change the structure of the situation to make it a joint problem, the more energy you will have for productive activities.

Reducing Client Ambiguity

Ironically, one of the best ways to clarify your own role is to help clients to clarify theirs. If you are both concerned with a quality service or product, and the relationship of that product to well-understood expectations is apparent, a discussion about roles will sharpen reciprocal expectations and identify areas of unnecessary ambiguity. As a helper, it pays to play an educator role, by teaching clients how to be effective (see Chapter 10). If you don't bother on the assumption that you shouldn't "have" to do it, then you are a significant contributor (by default) to the conflicting or unrealistic expectations. If you want them to help you do your best, you've got to consider client education as a legitimate means to that end.

Focusing on Your Own Learning

Promoting your own education can also be a means to reduced role ambiguity. Setting specific personal learning goals provides a structure for asking questions, for using experiences that might otherwise seem extraneous, and (if you learn something) for applying what you've learned to the way you shape your next role. A learning focus also can reduce ambiguity in the overall pattern of projects you work on, by providing criteria for choosing what to do next, or what type of client to seek. One of the most ambiguous situations is when you treat all projects as equally worthwhile, interesting, and educational, which is rarely true. It just *seems* that way unless you focus specifically on what you are (and want to be) learning from each project and from their pattern over time. This may sound quite abstract but I mean it concretely. This strategy won't be worth anything unless you consciously work out your learning goals, write them down, and monitor their progress.

Group Support

It is obviously not solely the individual's responsibility to manage the ambiguity in a consulting role. Staff units can define many of the hazy aspects, such as work hours and patterns, uses of confidential information, negotiating and ending projects, progress reports, and preferred areas for further personal development. These norms can provide structure for role behaviors even if those behaviors are irrelevant or inaccurate in the larger organization. In a sense, the staff group is providing a micro-world in which members know where they stand, even if they physically spend most of their time on other groups' territory.

Using Ambiguity

The previous strategies have generally emphasized clarifying, shaping, or sharpening situations so that role ambiguity is reduced and choices about actions can be evaluated more directly. A different but equally effective approach is to *use* the role ambiguity as a positive factor. Lack of structure or clear expectations allows for the freedom to experiment and set your own tone. This is especially useful in the scouting-entry phase, where you often need to do *something* to find out more about the client's needs and willingness to commit resources and attention. Yet it is not clear what the best "something" would be. A less rigid role allows enough slack for testing and exploring until you know enough to zero-in on a few key activities.

This approach is as much an emotional *attitude* as it is a planned strategy. This attitude, however, is easier for some people than for others. Some people can tolerate, and even seek out, role ambiguity as a feature of their work lives while others would like to have more structured, specified roles.

As nice as it is to have a choice and as reasonable as each stance is, the nature of internal consulting dictates that the consultant's role, even under the best of circumstances, will have some ambiguity. If ambiguity is highly stressful for you, perhaps you should not consult.

I say this for two reasons. The consulting process can be a continual problem if you are always feeling exposed, at risk, and vulnerable. As a result, your energy goes into clarifying roles and creating structure. On the other hand, reducing uncertainty is not necessarily a positive contribution to the project or the client. That is, it may be serving the consultant's emotional needs more than the client's work needs. This is why it is helpful to sharpen your role and reduce uncertainty in some situations and to relax and live with the ambiguity in others. Both are necessary options for your repertoire so that you may respond to a range of clients and client situations.

NOTES FOR CHAPTER 7

1. For a fuller discussion of the opportunities and difficulties of learning while in the consultant role, see "Learning from Consulting," in my book *Consulting for Organizational Change* (Amherst, Massachusetts: University of Massachusetts Press, 1975), pp. 11–33.

Exercising Personal Influence

83

In previous chapters we have examined what we affect (the organizations and groups where we do our work) and the context within which we work (the role expectations which shape our own performances). But even with systems and roles, our most immediate effects often hinge on how well we influence people face-to-face. This chapter will therefore consider how to do this.

This topic is particularly appropriate because the internal consultant must often rely on personal influence in order to make things happen: to get clients to share information, to get them to commit to a project, or to get support from colleagues and one's boss. When the line manager has recognized spheres where he can set standards, the internal staff person makes things happen through exercising personal influence. It is therefore worth knowing as much as we can about how we influence others. It is also helpful to recognize various influence modes that others exercise toward us, so that we can choose a response.

The Positive Power and Influence Model

There are many theoretical schemes that have been developed to describe the interpersonal influence process. The one that I have found to be the most concrete, practical, and clearly developed is the Positive Power and Influence (PPI) Model developed by Roger Harrison and David Berlew.[1] Their model has been developed through extensive experimentation and testing in training situations, so it is well-founded; and I have used it with success. As I describe this model, remember that it is meant to represent modes of face-to-face influence. Its behavioral categories are not summaries of all life's processes, nor does the model imply that you *ought* to influence people all the time. It is meant simply to provide an orderly view of the personal influence processes.

Harrison and Berlew place influence modes into four broad categories:

- Rewards and Punishments (R and P)
- Participation and Trust (P and T)
- Common Vision (CV)
- Assertive Persuasion (AP)

Their basic theory says that these four areas cover most encounters. Each mode is relatively effective as the situations change, and there is no "best" method. They have found, however, that people are not equally at home with all four categories. We develop preferences, according to ease, in one or more of the areas, which we then over-use (even when not particularly appropriate). As people have some success using a particular mode, they rely on it, and become still better at it while neglecting to develop their skills in other modes. With these assumptions in mind, let us consider each of the four areas of influence.

Using Rewards and Punishments

In using Rewards and Punishments, you are basically trying to create a perception in the other person's mind that something that they care about getting (or avoiding) hinges on whether they do something that you want them to do. Rewards and Punishments behaviors fall into three sub-categories: *prescribing goals and expectations* for someone's behavior, what you want them to do, or what standards you will use to determine how well it is done; *evaluating* behaviors as being acceptable or unacceptable, useful or not useful, good or bad; and providing *incentives and pressures* as a result of your evaluation—offering bargains, rewards, punishments, recognition—contingent upon whether the person has met your expectations.

Your actual rewards and punishments may be as grand as yearly bonuses when a subordinate has exceeded his agreed-upon goals or as mundane as a smile when he has stuck to an agenda which you have set. Therefore, there are opportunities to use R and P quite frequently, such as in structuring events, meetings, or trying to get people to participate. It need not be used solely through the organization's formal reward system. As we said in Chapter 3, anything you can control that someone else cares about can be given or withheld based on whether they meet your expectations.

To be effective, this influence mode needs actions in all three sub-categories. It is not very effective to arbitrarily evaluate someone when you have not been clear about your expectations. Similarly, it doesn't do much good, in the long run, to set expectations and provide evaluations but not follow through with appropriate incentives or pressures. People will learn that their behavior will not lead to any particular result, so they allow you less R and P influence. This does not mean that you cannot influence through other modes, but rather that the effects of using R and P will dwindle.

In my consultant training programs, participants often become indignant when I describe R and P. Since they don't use Rewards and Punishments as a means to influencing clients or colleagues, they believe it is irrelevant. The reasons they give for not using Rewards and Punishments are: (a) they don't control the necessary commodities (salaries, bonuses, job assignments, promotions; and (b) that it is an authoritarian way to influence and so shouldn't be used.

These reactions are interesting for several reasons. First, they represent an unnecessarily narrow view of how people use reinforcements to influence others' behavior. If you are trying to get a client to tell you more of what he expects your role to be, nodding your head when he does it, or saying "that's a good point," is using R and P. Saying that you expect people to arrive on time for a project briefing session is R and P too, as is complaining about those who arrive late. The point is that we all use R and P in our interpersonal transactions, since life is a give-and-take process; and each transaction can count as an influence on behavior. The commodities do not have to be a system's formal rewards.

The concern about R and P being authoritarian is valid but can be over-played, since the process only becomes that if the influence is one-way. If you are working with a client and each of you sets expectations for the other and follows-up, then what you have is a balanced influence relationship, not one in which someone dominates. In fact, if an internal consultant is not willing to recognize and use control over commodities that others care about, then clients and managers in the system are more likely (since they *do* use this mode) to be dominant.

For each of the four modes of influence, there are situations when its use is likely to be more effective and situations where it is unlikely to influence. Using Rewards and Punishments is more likely to be effective in these kinds of situations:

- The person being influenced has a strong desire or need for those things which you can control;
- You have the power to give and withhold rewards relative to the person you are trying to influence;
- The person you are trying to influence is insecure or uncertain and wants to be given direction and evaluation;

- You don't care much about building a long-term relationship;
- You are in a situation where you can see whether or not the person you are trying to influence does, in fact, do what you want him to do;
- You have the opportunity to evaluate and either give or withhold rewards within a short time after the other's actions.

Using Rewards and Punishments tends to be less appropriate in situations such as these:

- The person you are trying to influence sees R and P actions as illegitimate;
- You cannot actually deliver a reward if the person accepts your influence;
- You will not be around enough to know whether the person is meeting your expectations or standards;
- The other person has a strong need for independence and would therefore reject any situation that made him feel dependent.

We will also have a better feel for when R and P is useful after we have described the other three modes of influence.

Using Participation and Trust

Participation and Trust attempts to develop a feeling of acceptance and trust between the other person and you, so that he will feel that you have his interests at heart as well as your own.

There are several types of behavior that fall under this heading. *Personal disclosure* includes sharing your feelings with the other person, being open about things that reflect well or badly on yourself, and admitting your own mistakes, shortcomings, and lack of knowledge. All of these are signals to the other person that you are not trying to get them to take all the risks, but rather that you are willing to reveal yourself along with them. *Testing and expressing understanding* is primarily "reading back" to the person what you have heard of their ideas and feelings for the purpose of testing your own understanding. *Recognizing and involving others* includes asking for contributions or ideas, giving the other person credit for an idea, or building on what the other person has proposed.

The point of this influence mode, then, is toward developing the sense of collaboration between the other person and yourself, so that the person identifies his goals with yours and therefore will accept your influence as being in his own interest. This style tends to build connections. These are all behaviors that some managers will try to generate in an attempt to *look* participatory and trustworthy, but they usually fail. Unless you really are listening to the other person or really do disclose things about yourself, the phoney actions are easy to spot and will breed mistrust.

Using P and T behaviors is more effective when you need the other person's active commitment and involvement in what you're trying to do; when you will not be around to administer conditional rewards and punishments, and so must rely on the person complying with your wishes on their own; when you need real collaboration for the particular task; and when the other person will resent your attempts at one-way influence or control.

It is likely to be less effective to use Participation and Trust behavior when you are the best decision-maker and no real commitment of others is needed to make the project go; when you are set on a single course of action and really are *not* open to influence from the other person (in which case your P and T efforts will ultimately be exposed as phoney); when the other person expects you to be in the expert helping role and to provide answers, without collaboration; and when the situation is such that it is not really in the other person's best interests to cooperate with you.

Using Common Vision

The third influence category is the development of a "common vision," a shared picture of where you are headed, what you are trying to accomplish, and why it would be worthwhile for others to help. Developing a common vision has two main sub-categories of actions. *Generating a shared identity* highlights common values, interests, style; for example, "since we all care about education and the development of children's abilities, we should . . . ." It includes building group cohesion by referring to the things you have in common with group members. *Articulating exciting possibilities* includes generating images of what the future could be like, if we did such and such; describing the possibilities inherent in your particular group or organization; showing your own excitement or enthusiasm for what's to be done and where it will get you; and helping other people describe their own hopes and dreams.

There is also an important *non-verbal* component to effective use of CV behaviors. Keeping eye contact, using animated movements, being alert and sitting upright rather than relaxed and slouching, and physically moving around are all indicators that your own energy is, in fact, tapped by the vision you are trying to share.

In my experience with using the PPI influence model in consultant training programs, Common Vision tends to be the least utilized influence mode; and the participants often feel awkward and shy when trying to use it. I suspect that this is true for our society as a whole, and that we do not practice Common Vision activities as we grow up. On the other hand, the managers that I have worked with who really used this mode effectively have all shared one characteristic: they were hard workers who were committed to making things happen and who spent many hours thinking about future possibilities, and how these possibilities could be implemented. They worked at it all the time, so that the images they generated were substantive. They weren't just

trying to use Common Vision as a strategy, they really *had*
visions of the future and knew why everyone would benefit
from joint efforts. These people weren't necessarily smarter
(although others around them often thought so), but they
spent much time and energy working on ideas and approaches to problems they felt were worth solving.

Using CV approaches obviously is not the only way
of influencing, nor is it appropriate for all situations. It
tends to be more effective when you must influence a number of people to make what you want happen; when there is
a common set of values and interests; when your main purpose is to generate a commitment to action, without the
specific actions being too important; and when others identify with you and what you are trying to do.

Common Vision is harder to use when the other person mistrusts your intentions or values; when you are not
held in high regard by the other person; and when there are
no identifiable first steps which the other person can take
toward achieving CV, that is, when they can't see what you
actually want them to do.

Using Assertive Persuasion

The fourth and last major category is that of Assertive Persuasion. This is the mode of trying to use logic and
persuasion to "convince" the other person that what you
want them to do is the right, correct, or effective thing to do.
There are two sub-categories of AP behaviors. One is *proposing,* which is the putting forward of ideas, suggestions
about what should be done or how to proceed, and other
concepts which others are asked to accept. Then there is
reasoning for and against, where you present arguments,
facts, or data which support your position. You may also
use this in agreeing or disagreeing with others' facts or
reasoning.

Assertive Persuasion, unlike Common Vision, tends
to be a highly overdeveloped style in American work organi-

zations. It is so heavily used that people often think of it as synonymous with influence. Internal consultants are particularly susceptible to getting locked into using only AP influence behaviors, because they are expected to be specialists who "know" a technical area and should therefore be able to speak authoritatively. AP is a consistent pattern even though clients are, in fact, moved to action for many reasons (eagerness, felt need, liking the consultant, or fear of reprisals) which are only slightly related to the logic of a given argument.

Assertive Persuasion tends to be most effective when you are perceived as knowing what you're talking about; when you are seen as relatively objective and not selling something that doesn't relate to the client's needs; when you are the only source of the information; and when you know enough about the other person's situation to speak to specific needs. Assertive Persuasion tends to be less effective when the other person has a strong need to be independent and develop his own sense of competence; when you and the other person are competing; when the other person has strong opinions of what he should do; and when the other person doesn't feel valued or appreciated by you, or feels you are condescending or patronizing.

Influence "Profiles"

These then are the four broad approaches to face-to-face influence: using Rewards and Punishments, Participation and Trust, Common Vision, and Assertive Persuasion. People are obviously not pure "types," using only one mode of influence; and we tend to have "profiles," or consistent patterns in how we try to influence, such as being high on Assertive Persuasion and Rewards and Punishments and relatively low on Participation and Trust and Common Vision. There is not space to go into the various possible profiles here, so interested readers are invited to the materials by Berlew and Harrison (see note 1).

One point from their research should be mentioned here, though. They have found that our culture places different emotional headings on the different styles. R and P and AP tend to be what Harrison and Berlew call "hard-track" strategies based on pushing and aggressiveness, while P and T and CV tend to be "soft-track" strategies based on creating conditions to help the other person take action. Both are legitimate ways to influence (given the appropriate conditions), but people tend to be more comfortable with either hard-track or soft-track styles.

If you accept the assumption that being an effective influence requires some flexibility, the issue becomes, "Which track am I more comfortable with and likely to use too much, and how can I gain practice in my less comfortable influence modes?" This is exactly the point of the Positive Power and Influence workshops; they provide a structure for self-diagnosis and practice that leads to development of influence skills that cannot be otherwise attained.

Implications

There are a number of final points that I would like to emphasize before leaving this topic. There is no single "best" way to influence others. It depends on who you are, who the others are, and what the situation is like. It's a diagnostic question, not, as we sometimes make it, a moral one. We are usually too narrow in our use of influence behaviors, continuing to use favorite modes even in situations where they will not work.

Another issue which is implied in this chapter is whether you *want* to be influential and affect what somebody does with his time, energy, and resources. Staff specialists often feel like they would prefer to focus on the content of a project or task and ignore the potential impact on the clients; yet the reality is that as you do your work, you always have the potential for influence, and in some cases, it is necessary in order to get the clients to play their own roles effectively.

In thinking of your own potential influence on clients or colleagues, it is also helpful to think in terms of a *broad range* of behaviors that are worth influencing: what people talk about, whether they stay on track, when they provide feedback, who manages the meeting, and even where they sit. All of these actions contribute to the total flow of a project, and their cumulative impact can be as great as those of the "big" decisions such as setting budgets or hiring people.

A third point can help you be effective in these daily opportunities to influence others: there is no substitute for being clear in your own mind about *who* you are trying to influence and *what* you are trying to get them to do (commit funds to your project or stop talking for a few minutes to hear what you have been trying to say). If you don't have these points in mind, it's hard to be creative about what influence mode to use, and you will rely on whatever mode with which you usually feel comfortable.

You also may find that you tend to use different modes of influence with colleagues and fellow specialists. This is not surprising, especially at the beginning of a project when role expectations are unclear. The role shaping process is one context where a broader range of modes could be used. In terms of the helping process, internal staff specialists deal mostly in the content of problems, using Assertive Persuasion to convince clients about a course of action. Yet at the very beginning of a project, using Participation and Trust helps the clients see *who* they're being asked to rely upon, and Common Vision can help generate excitement about why they should bother in the first place. The appropriate influence mode will vary with stages of the project, as well as with your expert, resource, or process roles. The more you want to avoid dependency and use the process role, the more appropriate it is to use Participation and Trust and less appropriate to use Rewards and Punishments or to work exclusively with Assertive Persuasion.

Finally, although this really requires a detailed discussion, there is an obvious link between system power and face-to-face influence. A high position in the hierarchy usually carries with it the authority to control more commodities for Rewards and Punishment. It puts you into a position where it is legitimate for you to control structures, such as meetings and agendas, and you are, thus, more likely to have a forum in which to attempt Assertive Persuasion or to express a Common Vision. A high position in the system often leads to more contacts and, especially if you are a visible leader, these contacts are likely to generate more ideas for the future. Common Vision comes more easily, then, to someone in such a role. Being able to control boundaries by determining who talks to whom, or how space is laid out, shapes the very context of face-to-face influence, and it may determine whether you have any opportunity to influence people.

NOTES FOR CHAPTER 8

1. The material on PPI is paraphrased from papers by Berlew and Harrison. This model serves as the basis for a number of PPI training programs of varying lengths presented by Situation Management Systems, Inc., Plymouth, Massachusetts.

Dilemmas of
Doing Business

Five basic dilemmas are associated with internal consulting roles: helping or controlling, helping or selling, doing or learning, hiding your magic or sharing it, and taking risks or playing it safe. These are obviously not the only dilemmas internal consultants face, but they do have the greatest impact on what consultants do and how they feel about it. These dilemmas are described here so that readers will see them as a natural, *positional* experience and not simply the result of personal failings or strange perceptions. There may not be an answer to any of these dilemmas, but there are good and bad approaches.

Helping or Controlling

This is the most widespread and fundamental dilemma: Are you trying to help the clients do what they do, or are you trying to get them to do what you (or your bosses) think they should do? This dilemma arises from several possible situations. One is when you represent an area of specialized expertise, such as information processing systems and technology. Your mandate from the organization may be to help clients with their system needs, but you are also supposed to be an agent or force for high quality information systems in the total organization.

The most conflict-ridden form of this dilemma is to be a part of the corporate staff of a large company and be expected to (a) help various clients in the subsidiary units and (b) be a monitor or police officer who looks for problems and patterns that headquarters wants to know about in order to "control" unwanted deviations in performance.

This usually results in considerable role confusion for both the consultant and the client about where the consultant's vested interest lies. In response, the client may hold back either by not using the consultant at all or by not telling the consultant anything she doesn't want to get back to corporate headquarters. This in turn makes it very hard for an internal consultant to help with any of the client's important problems. Unfortunately, these are precisely the areas which are most troublesome and which the client is likely to find embarrassing. These problems imply that the unit can't handle its own issues, especially to corporate executives who often see such situations out of context and without any background.

This conflict is more or less intense depending on the expectations of the corporate executives and how visible the consultant is to this group. The more the executives believe that the corporate staff groups are essentially *their* resources, to be used as extensions of themselves, the more pressure there will be on the consultants to report to headquarters. The more the executives believe that the best use for corporate staff is to deal with the units' problems in the field, and that the staffs are the *units'* resources, the less pressure consultants will feel. Consequently, they will have more freedom to focus on the clients' needs.

The consultant has several options in this regard. The most obvious is to negotiate a role definition with the key executives. If you really want to function as a helper, then this stance should be discussed and agreed upon with the executive to whom the staff group reports. Most important, the costs of *not* taking this stance should be discussed. This will clarify the goals of staff group work, such as when to service the headquarters or to service the units.

The second important role negotiation is with the client group. Since they will naturally wonder where your allegiance lies and what headquarters expects, this is a topic that should always be raised and clarified early. You need to negotiate certain ground rules with the client: what you can do, what you are free to share with your colleagues or with corporate headquarters, and what expectations for information sharing you have of the client. It is important that you visibly deal with the *reality* in this process; if part of your mandate is to report periodically to corporate headquarters, then this should be said to the client, and the implications of this should be spelled out. Alternatively, you may clarify "confidential" topics that you will not discuss.

One thing seems clear: if you establish a confidential relationship with clients and then pass on information to headquarters, it will sooner or later come back to you. The client will find out, not open up to you, *and* will spread the word that you are a stooge for headquarters. This will reduce your ability to establish future relationships. It's better, then, to be honest about your relationships, so that you and the client can collaboratively determine how to proceed.

Selling or Helping

The second dilemma concerns the focus of your energy and attention: doing a job for the client or selling your future services. This is not a particularly unique conflict, since professional people must sell themselves in order to survive. There are two situations which are more problematic—first, if your staff group or consulting unit is required by the company to "bill" its time, in either real dollars or overhead transfers, producing considerable pressure to justify the existence of the staff unit by billing as many of the total available person-hours as possible; second, when the client's *requests* do not match the *need*, as you see it.

The first case may lead to such non-client-oriented choices as: agreeing to do work that could actually be done better by another group or by an outside consultant; always choosing to spend time on billable activities rather than mixing development, training, evaluation, staff team development, and other long-term activities; and providing "help" in such a manner that the client continues to need your services when he might otherwise have become self-sufficient. In the second case, unrealistic requests can sometimes be rationalized by assuming that "the client knows best," even though we are uneasy and don't really think they are getting the best value for their time, attention, and money.

There is nothing inherently negative in selling services. It requires discipline, so as to provide a factor that keeps specialists focused on needs and satisfactions of their clients. The problem starts when the need to sell takes precedence over the client's needs. Eventually, such a position will become common knowledge, and you (or your group) will acquire a bad image. You will be seen as having a vested interest in pushing clients without regard for the technical merits of a project or just waiting a while to see what happens. This image will work against your ability to sell services.

I believe that the best route to selling your services, in the long run, is to provide high-quality services. You can, however, increase the probability that doing good work will lead to future projects. Be visible. Encourage potential clients to talk to previous ones, prepare and distribute written summaries which discuss the general benefits of the collaboration.

Work on role shaping, both for your group and yourself. Define expectations which might include: doing high quality work, even if it is at reduced volume; working at a good diagnosis of client's needs as a real service in itself, even if it results in a smaller project; and having a broad impact on the workings of the organization including unbilled as well as billable contacts. Organizational leaders who treat their staff groups as if they were profit centers miss the point: internal consultants are available and conversant with what's going on in the system so that they can respond rapidly to the needs of other units. This requires some freedom and doing tasks that are not for sale.

Doing or Learning

There is an implicit tension caused by being expected to bill clients for as many days as possible. The system's need to see you as "busy" and "productive" pushes you away from spending time on activities that do not look like work but are teaching you something. These less visible activities include sharing experiences and cases with colleagues, talking about process with clients, reading theory or related experiences, organizing problem-oriented forums as learning vehicles, and just making notes and thinking about what you are doing and how you are doing it.

It is hard to charge a client for most of these work modes which may, therefore, be seen as "luxuries." They are, however, necessities if your role includes serving current clients well and learning from the experience for future clients. With this in mind, the head of a staff group should actively set expectations (for the client and executives) which include learning activities as well as on-line delivery of services. This is a role for which one must work—it won't develop on its own!

Hiding Your Magic or Sharing It

All specialists who work with non-specialists share this question: How much do I reveal about *how* I do my stuff and how do I share it in such a way that clients can do parts of it themselves? We all want to be seen as unique, with special talents or knowledge that no one else has. The internal consulting role allows us to play this out, producing ideas or products, hoping, as the Wizard of Oz did, that no one will come behind the curtain and see how mundane our work really is. Still, the clients are not usually equipped to understand the complexities and subtleties of our field, without time and effort. Nor do they particularly care about gaining this specialized knowledge; they have their own business.

On the other hand, we do want the client to improve his ability in our area of expertise; and in fact this is one of the most obvious indicators that our work has made some difference. This dilemma is one we must live with, but I think most internal staff people lean more than is necessary toward the hiding end rather than regularly sharing their working styles.

Ultimately, the tension between hiding and sharing is best resolved by referring to the goals of the project and therefore to the expectations for the consultant's role. The stronger the emphasis on the process role, the more you are trying to develop the client's ability to diagnose and solve his own problems, without remaining dependent on the consultant. This speaks strongly for sharing both background and modes of working with the client as you go, so that he learns from the experience. The stronger the emphasis on the expert role and the more the project is defined as getting a task done competently, the less you share. In fact, such behavior might be seen as intrusive or time-wasting. Whichever direction you go, *choosing* a direction should be a collaborative process between you and the client, so that you have similar expectations.

Being Safe or Taking Risks

How much should we rely on those things that we already know how to do well and about which we can predict the outcome? How much should we risk when the consequences are unknown? Our need for some security and stability leads us not to take risks, whereas the need for excitement and for making major changes encourages us to try things, even when they may backfire.

There are four sources of risk that are associated with the internal consulting role such as:

- *Power differentials* between consultant and client or consultant and superior. If something goes wrong, each of these powerful groups can affect such things as the con-

sultant's job (having one or not), career (having success-
fully developed within the organization), image (in the
eyes of other power people), or resources (such as a budget
for future work).

- *Uncertainty of outcome* comes when a situation is complex and the only way to find out more about it is to do
something which will then get a reaction. The outcome
may be one you like or one you don't like; and you may
also be faulted for not having known in advance what the
outcome would be.

- *Personal embarrassment* is something that most of us try
to avoid, and feel bad about when it happens. We feel em-
barrassed when we fail, when we have looked foolish in
others' eyes, or when we disclose something about ourselves which others find to be silly or stupid.

- *Violating peer norms* such as the general rules by which
our colleagues perform professional tasks can be a major
risk. The norms can be about anything—style, dress,
political values, commitment to the consulting team, time
of arrival at work—and at times these norms will conflict
with what you believe is the most effective behavior on a
project. These are the times when you have to decide how
much risk to take.

One of the most prevalent types of high risk situations is when your professional expertise leads you to favor
one course of action, and the norms of the wider organization dictate that you should not. The risk is felt in terms of
image, career, relationships with powerful people, embarrassment if you take a chance and it doesn't work out, and
loss of the acceptance of the people around you. It might
help readers to assess their own style by evaluating which of
these are the most threatening and which are calculated risks
that can be taken easily. Once you know the biggest risks,

ask: What are the risks of *not* taking action in those situations? These risks are not as conspicuous and often are overlooked.

What can be done to deal with the safety/risk dilemma? There are two approaches to reduce this tension. One is to use the role-shaping process, incorporate some freedom to take chances, and have it be taken as part of your basic business. This includes defining your role with a client as someone who is of value precisely because you are *not* exactly like him: you see and deal with problems differently and that should be expected. A similar role-shaping process should be used with your boss and other key executives, in which you highlight the value to the organization of employing staff people who do not simply replicate the values and norms of the traditional line organization.

If done well, this process can reduce the risks associated with bold moves. The second strategy is to change the way you *feel* about risks, to accept the consequences of actions that don't pan out. In fact, an internal consultant will generally not be a potent force until he or she can accept the possibility of having "the worst" happen—losing the job, failing on a project, looking foolish—and feel that it would not be the end of the world. The freedom that this feeling brings will often mean you become less tense, better able to act when it is important, and more likely to succeed when you do take chances, thus reducing the actual risks.

In sum, these five dilemmas have been selected from many possibilities. These are the tensions that have been described most often and represent a major stress when doing business as a helper inside an organization. I have suggested several strategies, the main one being to work on role-shaping processes *early* in a project with clients, colleagues, and people above you. Setting expectations can allow room in your role for taking time out to learn, working for the client in a confidential manner, worrying less about billing your time, and taking risks that will be supported by boss and colleagues. In the end, though, there will always be dilemmas in the internal consulting role and they must be accepted as part of the territory.

NOTES FOR CHAPTER 9

1. If these issues are of particular interest or concern to you, I recommend "Learning from Consulting," in my book, *Consulting for Organizational Change* (Amherst, Massachusetts: University of Massachusetts Press, 1975), pp. 11–33.

Mundane but Important Consulting Skills

This book is based on the premise that having specialized professional knowledge is not automatically the same thing as knowing how to help other people cope better with problems in your area of expertise. An "expert" may be a good, bad, or mediocre consultant, just as he may be a good, bad, or mediocre teacher. Special helping skills are needed in order to make practical use of your technical skills.

The previous chapters have focused on what I consider to be some of the most important skills for internal helpers: designing change processes; diagnosing and intervening in human systems; analyzing and shaping one's roles in relation to clients; and influencing other people effectively by using appropriate methods. This chapter briefly surveys some other areas of specific helping skills. These are recurring tasks that a staff specialist ought to do well to be considered a professional consultant. The following discussions provide the mechanics for being a helpful staff member in an organization. The intent of this chapter is to define and describe these skill areas as a basis for future learning efforts: attending development sessions; getting feedback from clients, colleagues, or bosses; reading about the area in more detail; and designing personal projects which provide practice in selected activities. Reading about these topics is, of course, not the same thing as becoming better trained in them, it simply points the way.

Diagnosing Problems in the Helping Process

Most staff specialists presumably have some background and competence in diagnosing problems. Where diagnostic competence is more problematic, however, is in the helping process itself: being able to spot, identify, analyze, and understand difficulties in serving the needs of a client. This diagnostic skill can have a high payoff, since it is used to affect the consulting process itself, and therefore, how well your technical diagnostic skills can be applied.

There are a number of ways in which to be a good diagnostician. One is spotting problem *patterns* as they build, rather than just noticing how single events go. Noticing patterns means remembering how a number of similar events transpired, and then generalizing about these events as a class. One must also recognize those issues that seem to have been resolved but, in fact, *recur*. This is almost always a sign that you have either not diagnosed the causes correctly or have been defining the wrong problem.

There can be any number of problems in the helping process: difficulties in getting information from a client; an inability to get any program follow-up, even when the client claims to be committed; consistently failing to meet client's expectations (or the reverse); confusions over decision-making responsibilities and authorities; and an imbalance in energy, so that the consultant always has to initiate action. These situations are indicated by experiences: you feel vaguely uneasy each time you go to the client's offices; you feel tense when proposing that a task be done by a certain date (as if it were a favor or an imposition, rather than a natural part of the project); you find yourself feeling pessimistic, even though the project appears to be right on target in terms of technical accomplishments; your time scale for scheduling events seems to be out of synchronization; you feel tired at the end of each client contact, as if you had been "switched on" all day. Even though you can't put a name or label to it, this instinctive uneasiness is usually a good barometer as to how the process is going, and should be used to stimulate a more formal study (with the client) of how the process is being managed. Although this may sound obvious, my observations suggest that internal consultants often push aside such intangible indicators as not being relevant to the task, or as personal failings, rather than being indicative of problems with the project's structure and process.

Another point to remember is to start with *problem statements*, "We're not up to date on what we're each doing," rather than with *solution statements*, "We need more regular meetings with each other." So-called problem diagnosis often begins with an implied solution (as in "more meetings") which makes it difficult to discover alternative solutions or to spot any but the obvious causes. It is especially true in the area of process problems that time spent identifying *causes* rather than jumping to solutions will be time well spent, even though it is a slower process. It focuses energy and attention on the issues that can really make a difference, not just on superficial causes.

Another aid to diagnosing problem causes is an applied behavioral science model called the "force-field" analysis. Its basic assumption is that most patterns of behavior are the result of a dynamic field of forces, some pushing toward (driving) more of the behavior and some pushing away from (blocking) it. When you're in a situation where you would like someone to be behaving differently, drawing a simple diagram of driving and blocking forces can help you to sort out the causes of the blockage and to identify the ones on which you can act.[1]

Designing and Managing Meetings

Of all the activities of modern organizational life, none is more prevalent than the meeting. Whether it's two people or twenty, a large amount of the energy in an organization is channeled into meetings. The work of internal consultants is no exception. Although solitary tasks may be associated with a project, there are also times when you need to get people together in order to do something: describe the client's needs, define the project and contract, collect information during the project, share results and evaluate progress, or gain commitment for next steps. It is, therefore, critical for an internal consultant to be skilled in designing and conducting meetings.

It is important to make more conscious choices about meeting design and conduct, although this is usually done in "traditional" or assumed ways. A successful meeting, whether it's two people talking for fifteen minutes in a client's office or twelve people together for three hours in a formal conference room, should have at least a chosen shape and a planned scenario (even if that scenario is to get people together and see what happens). Since there are quite a few points to be made, they are summarized in the following outline.

NOTES ON MEETINGS MANAGEMENT

I. Creation/Design of the Meeting

  A. What's the *purpose*? (Be clear about this, although it can be changed by discussion.)
    The main possibilities:
    Information-sharing
    Problem-finding
    Problem-solving
    Decision-making
    Testing/Sensing issues or
    Some combination (often tricky unless changes of topic are clearly handled)

  B. Is the meeting *necessary,* or can it be done another way? (in notes or phone calls)

  C. Is it *regular* (recurring) or special? If regular, does it need altering or re-charging somehow? Has the meeting format gone stale?

D. *Who* should attend?
Likely criteria:
Who has needed information?
Who has ownership/stake in outcome?
Who will have to follow-up if action becomes necessary as a result from the meeting?
Who has position/power to affect outcome?
Who has energy/interest in the topics?
Criteria should be chosen with regard to purposes of the meeting.

E. *When* should it happen?
Are there time pressures that might make it hard for people to attend?
What will come before and after? (Will the meeting occur in the middle of a flow of events?)
Have you asked the participants about their schedules? Do you know of events that will pose a conflict for them?
Is the timing, in the day or week, thought through? (Monday morning or Friday afternoon are usually not great meeting times, except for special purposes.)
What are the high-energy times in this organization?

F. What *location* should be used?
Does it suit the purpose?
Materials available?
Information available?
Interruption control?
Symbolic messages?
Flexibility needed in terms of layout?

G. *Pre-meeting* events:

   Agenda solicited and/or shaped in advance?

   Information gathered?

   Issues identified?

   Other (for high-leverage use of the actual meeting time)

II. Managing the Meeting

   A. *Start on time.* (Don't "train" people to be late by making a habit of waiting for latecomers.)

   B. Start by *reviewing* purposes, who is here and why, and how long the meeting will probably last or is set to run. (Don't assume "we all know this already." It only takes a few seconds to confirm this if true, and it's well worth finding out if you don't all have the same expectations.)

   C. *Review the agenda:* Set priorities with a rough time allotment, and place each item in sequence. (Don't be at the mercy of an original random order.)

   D. *Specify processes* to be used during the meeting (discussion, reporting, questioning, or brainstorming).

   E. If decisions will be made, clarify *how.*

   F. In general, the leader should try to *minimize ambiguity* over the structure and process of the meeting.

   G. Monitor the *relevance* of contributors and keep them on the topic unless there is a conscious switch.

   H. Try to *avoid long speeches and monologues;* they tend to enervate most groups.

   I. *Test* for whether *silent members* have contributions to make (without requiring that they make ritual inputs).

J. *Keep track* of points, decisions, and who will do what by when. (Do this *visibly,* such as on newsprint pad, to stimulate discussions that build on previous points.)

K. Be crisp about *finishing* a discussion or making a transition to another topic instead of dragging on or shifting accidentally.

L. *End meetings on time* if possible, or make a *conscious decision* to continue, do not just drift into it.

M. Try to end with some clear notion of *what happens next.* Even if that is to be nothing, say so.

III. Evaluation Processes, Learning to Do Better

A. Build in time to *critique* at the end.

B. Be willing to talk about what is *actually happening* (even though it may sound critical).

C. Use evaluations to help *plan* and *start* the next session or meeting.

D. Use *specific* dimensions, such as:

Clarity of purpose?

Degree of participation?

Amount of energy and interest?

Did we accomplish our tasks?

Amount of openness, frankness?

How influence was distributed?

Use of time?

Was the meeting necessary?

Did we stay on track?

Were we clear about our roles (at least the more formal ones)?

IV. Specific Values and Group Norms that Promote Meeting Effectiveness

A. If you are trying to make a particular meeting go very well, then the above points can help.

B. If you want to improve the whole *pattern* of meetings that you and/or clients hold, then you need to do something additional: promoting certain values and group norms which support the mode of working.

The meeting is "owned" in part by all who are there, not just by the boss or formal leader, and all members therefore share responsibility for having the meeting go well.

We should manage the meeting process consciously and make open decisions if we change the process in the middle.

High disclosure, that is, having few taboo topics will encourage real discussions rather than just going through the motions.

We should listen to each other and not interrupt.

There should be no side conversations.

We should have concern for and trust each other so that agreements and disagreements can both be expressed in an atmosphere of collaboration.

V. Some Consequences of Using Effective Meeting Skills

A. Use time better in meetings.

B. Get better information sharing.

C. Combine talents and efforts better.

D. Have fewer unnecessary meetings.

E. Exercise conscious control of the process (rather than unconscious drifting).

F. Open the possibility of playing different roles in a meeting, so people don't get stereotyped.

G. Enjoy meetings more, and feel more awake and alive.

This is a very condensed list of the considerations leading to better meeting management. How you apply it, however, depends on your role in the meeting. There are several natural roles that an internal consultant is likely to be playing in a meeting: convener and chairperson; convener but not chairperson; participating member; critiquing observer; and silent observer. It helps to have a clear image of what you believe an effective meeting to be, regardless of *your* role (although you can usually have more impact in the more active roles). Still, a good member will improve a meeting's process if he or she can diagnose what's wrong and feels responsible for its improvement. Not knowing what's better and not caring about influencing are two sure ways to be an irrelevant member.

Preparing and Using Reports

Readers will probably feel that I have now turned completely back to old ground when I raise the topic of becoming better at preparing and using reports. In fact, most readers have considerable competence in report preparation, especially in their areas of expertise. On the other hand, I also believe that reports can too easily become an automatic response—we do them because they should be done and in the way we've always done them. I would like to suggest some questions about the use of reports so as to keep from getting into a rut and to utilize their full potential.

The Report as Product: Although we often treat reports as written documents, there are many possible forms a report can take: written paper, slide show, film strip, model, oral presentation, demonstration exercise, and a set of questions to which the client must respond. The key is to ask why we are doing the report and what form would best serve that purpose.

Clarifying Goals: Choosing a form implies that you know why you are doing a report at all. Are you trying to summarize progress, test your own results, stimulate clients to action, stir their interests, justify the costs of your help by providing a tangible product, or give closure to a project? Each of these are legitimate reasons for doing a report, but they are best accomplished by different forms. The report can also have a symbolic function: to make a concrete *thing* out of a set of ideas or concepts. Clients will often be unimpressed by your recommendations until they are recorded and can be discussed formally.

Receivers of the Report: A very important choice, which is often made in an offhand manner, is who should receive a particular report. Again, this often is a stereotyped procedure based on client system norms about who has positional "rights" to get it. And yet, this decision *should* hinge on your purposes in doing the report. In some cases, you may want to push for a larger distribution than the client would. The point is that it is part of your business to guide where the report goes and who has access. In Chapter 3, we defined receivers as a systemic intervention, and you can create new groupings or structures by the pattern of who gets your report. You also make a symbolic statement about roles by whom you define as receivers and non-receivers.

Combinations: One of the most critical choices about a report's use is what else to do with it besides just writing it: holding a formal presentation; preparing auxiliary data summaries; setting up discussions; and designing a plan whereby people become familiar with the report, come together to discuss it, and come back together later to make action decisions. The point is that if you are an internal helper then producing the report is not your goal, it is a means to an end. Doing the report in a vacuum, without designing a process for how it can be used, is like producing half a play and hoping that the audience develops a second half that fits with the first. You should not leave the decisions regarding the report to the client's good intentions.

Figure 10.1. A Client Report Checklist

- What are my goals for doing reports?
- For this particular report?
- What should I include and leave out?
- What's the best timing for recurring periodic reports? For special ones?
- Does the client system have a poor history in using reports?
- Can I help them do better with mine?
- What form will be best for the impact I'm seeking?
- .Must it look like other reports?
- What norms are there about reports in this system?
- Which norms do I want to satisfy, and which ones do I want to violate?
- In terms of project flow, where is this report?
- What do I want to have happen next, and what should we do in connection with the report in order to help this to happen?
- Who should get the report, and in what form?
- Should there be a difference in when people get it?

Educating the Clients

Another neglected skill area, that I will only touch on, is educating clients: helping them to better use your help as well as other resources inside and outside the system. The typical internal staff consultant seems to spend half her time lamenting the lack of ability found in the line organization's members. The trap is that consultants can take the clients' attitudes and skills toward them as givens, assuming that they either have a positive stance or they don't.

It would be better to include in your role definition educating the clients in how to use you well, what you can do, how they should seek out problem patterns, what information they should share with you so that you will know when to take action, or how and when to provide you with

reactions to you. This educative function should be negotiated early during the original role-shaping discussions, so
that clients will see it as legitimate for you to help them
become better clients. The initiative will most likely have to
come from you, because it's unlikely that clients would generate such a request.

In some instances you may find it worth your time to
educate a client group in some of the basic ways of thinking
about your specialty. For example, if you are an information systems specialist, some of these ways of thinking which
might not be natural to the clients include automatically
assessing the quality of information, creating data bases,
taking advantage of easy information access and retrieval,
and thinking, in terms of probability, about events and their
inferences. A clear option exists here: you can decry the fact
that they don't know how to use your skills, or you can help
them become better at it.[2]

Being Helped by Others

The last skill is more of an attitude toward your work
rather than a concrete skill. It is the ability to use and be
helped by the resources around you. This may seem like
another point that can be taken for granted, but it is also
one that I think internal staff specialists do not use. Regularly playing helping roles inside an organization can make
you very comfortable with being the expert. However, this
role gives you little practice in being helped by someone else;
and over time you can lose the ability to comfortably accept
help. Since it feels like you are one-down when someone
tries to help you, you avoid such situations.

This pattern of being the helper also leads to a feeling
of discomfort about *asking* for help from others, as if this
were an admission of weakness or incompetence. Specialists
are supposed to know answers, especially if you are pushed
toward the expert role mode by your client or boss. And yet
we always counsel clients to be more creative in recognizing,

seeking, and using the resources in the system. Readers may be saying to themselves right now, "Sure, I know that and I do it all the time." Unfortunately, it is not so. There is room for most consultants to practice identifying and seeking out resources that might improve their work. This is especially true when setting up natural feedback processes so that clients can help you do your job better. But first, you must publicly admit that it is *possible* to do your job better.

NOTES FOR CHAPTER 10

1. For a fuller discussion of Force-Field diagrams in diagnosing change process problems, see D. Kolb, I. Rubin, and J. McIntyre, *Organizational Psychology: An Experiential Approach* (Englewood Cliffs, New Jersey: Prentice-Hall, 1971), pp. 305–309.

2. Readers interested in this should see "Learning and the Client's Role," in my book, *Consulting for Organizational Change* (Amherst, Massachusetts: University of Massachusetts Press, 1975), pp. 34–43.

Internal and External Consulting Roles

One sentiment has run through many of my training programs: the participants feel that internal consultants or
specialists (employees of the organization whose members
they help) work at a disadvantage. Such employees are
treated with far less deference, respect, and credibility than
are their external counterparts. Internal people speak re-
sentfully and wistfully about the ease with which external
people sell their services, even when internal people can't
give the same services away.

So it is a good idea to discuss this feeling and try to
look at the differences in the internal and external helping
roles more objectively. As you might expect, we find that
each case actually includes positive and negative factors.
Some of these factors are related to either the external or internal position, while other features are rather arbitrary.

Comparing the internal and external consultant
roles often helps workshop participants to see their internal
roles more clearly and to recognize advantages to which
they had not paid attention or used well. We also define the
features of the external role which would be quite useful for
an internal consultant, even if such notions break with
tradition.

Advantages of Internal Consultant Roles

The internal consultant has a number of distinct advantages over the external role which fall into four general
areas: job security, information about the organization, an

"insider" image, and continuity of work and experience in the system.

Security

■ You have a regular paycheck and a place to work every day; your uncertainty is lower.

■ Professional expertise leads to some security within the system and, if need be, in getting another job.

■ Many potential clients are available without having to do massive marketing efforts.

■ If the support of top people is available, you can have entree to many parts of the organization as their representative.

Information about the Organization

■ You often know whom to call or see in order to make something happen.

■ You know how budgets and other administrative procedures work.

■ You can identify key decision-makers or influentials for particular issues.

■ You know the organization's history and its typical problems, patterns, and attempted solutions.

■ You are knowledgeable about the power and politics of the system, so that you have a sense of place and timing for your work.

Image as an Insider

■ You are seen by the clients as "one of us," with mutual interests; this can generate a comfortable feeling, especially at the beginning of a project.

■ You "know the ropes" and are seen therefore as a potential source of advice to clients on how to get things done.

- You are seen as accessible—easy to contact and available for scheduling.
- If you are part of an internal staff group, the group's image allows potential clients to feel some confidence, even if they have not worked with you personally.

Continuity of Work and Experiences

- Follow-up activities or projects can be designed to build on earlier efforts; you are around to sense when this is appropriate.
- You have access to the client organization for long enough to see results, get feedback, and learn from your experiences.
- Word of your activities usually gets around and you can build on your successes.
- The clients see you as likely to be available for continued support—you will not "abandon" them as external consultants might.

Disadvantages of Internal Consultant Roles

The disadvantages or constraints of the internal role fall in three areas: negative aspects of the "insider" image, costs of accessibility (that go along with the advantages), and dependence on one organization.

The Insider Image

- It's more difficult to have credibility as an expert (prophet without honor in his own land).
- You may be seen as so close to one group that you will not provide "objective" help to the clients because you might have an axe to grind.

- You may be a member of a staff group that has a reputation based on earlier history and performance, even though this image has little to do with the roles you are now trying to perform.
- You are seen as "just one of us," not special, and are taken for granted, with less attention paid to how you use your time and energy.

Accessibility to Clients

- You are relatively easy to get in touch with and are expected to be responsive, so that your energy may be absorbed in many small but inconsequential demands.
- It is sometimes hard to have a crisp ending to a project.
- The visibility you have in the system doesn't just include successes. It also holds for "failures" and tough experiences.
- It is often easier to blame the internal consultant for difficulties than the external one, since you are a handy scapegoat.
- If clients are not charged money directly for your services, which are available on an "as needed" basis, your work may be undervalued.

Dependence on One Organization

- Although you have the advantage of a regular paycheck, you also have the threat of losing your only source of income if you have a confrontation with a client or boss.
- You may be caught in a squeeze between what a loyal member of the organization should do and what an effective specialist in your professional area should do.
- Your actions are often controlled by people in power who know little about good professional practices in your area.

In summary, internal consulting roles are seen (by people who are in them) as having advantages and disadvantages stemming from the same factors: accessibility between clients and consultant, which provides contacts but may breed contempt; the security of a job, which also implies the risk of losing it; and the continuity and image of being an insider, which also allows for some scapegoating and stereotyping.

Advantages of the External Consultant Role

As you might expect, the features of the external consultant role mirror those of the internal. The advantages stem from the "outsider" image, not being dependent on one organization, clearer separation of consultant from client, and clearer contracts.

The Outsider Image

- You (usually) have a reputation as an "expert" in your field.
- You must be good in order to survive as a consultant.
- You are usually seen as relatively objective and removed from specific cliques or political battles.
- Your distance from the day-to-day experience of clients makes you seem more remote and mysterious.
- You often get better cooperation and consideration from clients when you schedule events, since your presence is seen as special and your time as limited.

Non-Dependence on One Organization

- Your livelihood is not tied to success on any one project.
- You have greater freedom to accept or reject a project.

- You can give a project your best professional shot, not compromise your integrity, and leave it if it doesn't work out.
- You can sell the same product to several organizations, since you are not limited to one market.
- You can make more money (disputed by several external consultants).

Clearer Separation from the Client

- Projects are more clearly defined; you don't drift into them.
- You are not necessarily expected to be constrained by all the norms and traditions that apply to members of the system.
- It is often easier to cleanly end a project, since you are not physically present for casual follow-up requests.
- You may have access to more information and resources outside the boundaries of the client organization.
- The relative failure of a particular effort is not so visible to other current/potential client systems.

Clearer Contracts

- A client is more conscious of giving you specific authority and support.
- Your costs are consciously decided upon by the client, who is usually (but not always) paying for your work directly; you are not paid in "funny money" transfers as are internal groups.
- There is often a need for a more formal budget and contract in order to obtain higher management's approval; this is a good discipline for clarifying contract issues early

Disadvantages of the External Role

There are fewer disadvantages in the external role than for the internal, but they fall into two related areas: lack of connection with the organization and distance from the client.

Lack of Connection to the System

- You are dependent on internal people for your connection and support within the system.
- If you are dismissed as a consultant, you can't really stay around to spot other opportunities to accomplish something you think needs doing. (An internal person may still be working with nearby client groups and can get another chance.)
- It may not be legitimate for you to contact people in the system who you believe can make something happen, and you will be seen as just trying to "peddle your product" if you do so.
- You may be seen as "not our kind," as being different from the client, and not really having his interests at heart. You make him uncomfortable because you are an outsider.

Distance from the Client

- You may be working on a project and not see that conditions in the system are changing significantly so that you should alter your approach.
- You may not be around enough to see the *patterns* in client's problems, so that you work too much on isolated symptoms and not enough on causes.
- You may not have the opportunity to see the results or effects of your efforts, which makes it hard to learn.
- Successes in one organization are not apparent to potential clients without considerable effort on your part.

For the external role, then, the perceived advantages and disadvantages both stem from the formal separation of consultant from client system, providing degrees of freedom but also some blocks in information, access, and empathy between client and consultant. It is also interesting to note that none of the internal consultants in my programs mentioned lack of security as a disadvantage of the external role, even though other external consultants attest that the necessity to hustle for work and to remain calm when there isn't much work around can be a significant energy drain. Independence generally doesn't come for free.

Improving the Internal Role

When we consider these advantages and disadvantages, a natural question is raised: How can an internal consultant increase advantages and reduce the disadvantages? This is, in fact, easy to do, since so much of this depends on attitude. That is, an internal consultant who pays a good deal of attention to role analysis and conscious role-shaping with her clients is likely to operate with many of the advantages which we attribute to the external role.

Within this general framework, there are ten strategies that I have found helpful in expanding the internal consultant's freedom to act professionally. They don't all work all the time, but they change your role instead of leaving it to organization forces.

■ The most important strategy is to decide that, if you must, you could live without the organization. If you really feel that way, you will be less hesitant to take necessary risks. This, in turn, is likely to make you more effective, and ironically, more likely to remain if it is a system where professional effectiveness is valued.

■ An aid to living with leaving is to identify your security with your professional expertise rather than with having

an unblemished career pattern within the particular organization. The former is called a "cosmopolitan" stance,
while the latter is referred to as a "local" approach. A
cosmopolitan's reference group is composed of professional colleagues, while a local's consists of members of a
home organization.

- The most explicit strategy is early, distinct role-shaping
activities between (a) your boss, (b) your clients, and yourself. This implies the possibility that you might say "no" to
a project when a suitable contract cannot be negotiated,
just as an external consultant might do.

- One of the most important early contract subjects is to
sharpen the client's view of the direct and indirect costs to
be incurred. This starts the process off on a healthy foot-
ing and can avoid unnecessary low priority activities.
External consultants know how much time they would
waste if they didn't screen out less serious prospects,
especially in the scouting process.

- One way of keeping an image of objectivity is to avoid
becoming connected with only one faction within a di-
vided client system. An advantage of being inside the
organization is that you often know what the divisions
are; and you should use this information to insure you are
connected across factional lines, not just within one sub-
group.

- When you are caught in a squeeze between conflicting expectations, such as when your boss negotiates a contract
for you with a client group's boss, you should be willing to
call the basic structure into question just as an external
consultant would. At the very least you need to acknowledge that you know your clients are "captive," and to
show that you are willing to work toward an agreed mode
of working which actually does serve their needs.

- Another key aspect of conscious role management is to set clear expectations about how a project will end, with either a clean break or with continued support over a specified period of time. Either way you are trying to reduce the energy drain of being perceived as automatically accessible and responsive on demand without any commitment on the client's part.

- Although it may not be your area of expertise, you might also try improving the norms and climate of your organization concerning the value placed on internal helping resources. Or encourage someone who specializes in such work to deal with it.

- There are certain projects where you probably would have the most effect by teaming up with an external consultant, forming an inside-outside team that can take advantage of both the image of distance/specialness and the savvy of knowing the system. This can work well *if* both of you role-shape so that neither lets the client's attraction to a more mysterious resource eclipse what *you* have to offer.

- Last, you may use a strategy related to the basic role question, internal or external to what? Although you may be part of a staff group that is part of the same organization as your client, you may structure your relationship to the whole so that you appear to be an external consultant. This structuring includes having your offices at another physical location, having no administrative links to the higher executive structure, and establishing the staff group's mission and goals such that they are protected from political influences. These moves will help clients feel that, while you are technically a member of the organization, you are distant enough to be objective and free to do your best.

What Role Do You Want?

All of these strategies can expand the internal consultant's freedom of action and ability to be effective in working with client groups. A question still remains, however, of what type of position you would most like to have. To this end I have prepared a summary table (Figure 11.1) which expands the role comparison to two tensions: internal versus external and staff helping versus line managing positions. As you can see, these two choices create four types of positions: (A) internal staff consultants, (B) external consultants, (C) internal line managers, and (D) external regulatory agents. (I included (D) because, although not "consultants" *per se*, such agents are expected to influence what people do in organizations and, in a broad sense, are held accountable for consequent behavior. This places them between internal managers and external consultants.) Each role includes particular factors which increase or decrease the employee's ability to take necessary actions and risks.

The question then becomes not a systemic one (What are these roles like in an organization, and how can they be shaped better?) but a personal one. In which type of position do I function best and how will I choose to do my work? Do you want some security, connection, and system norms which go with the internal role; or would you rather work at a distance, with more freedom, some insecurity, and a greater emphasis on building trust? Neither is the "right" answer, and the choice is one that individuals can only make for themselves. I do hope, however, that it is clear that many of the assumed differences between internal and external roles are more a function of the typical (relatively unconscious) role-shaping process than a function of inherent structural differences. As such, expectations can be altered to provide internal consultants more of the advantages of outside ones; and, for that matter, external consultants can pay more attention to organizational norms.

Figure 11.1. Features of the Internal-External and Consultant-Manager Role Differences

	Consultant Helpers	Line Managers
Internal to the Organization	*Influence Factors:* (+) know the system (+) availability, accessibility (+) specialist point of view (−) familiarity (−) career or job dependence (A) INTERNAL STAFF *Main Risks:* * not being responsive * not being helpful * making trouble by being too confronting	*Influence Factors:* (+) have legitimate, positional authority (+) know the system (−) view from one spot (−) constrained by job expectations, hard to experiment (C) MANAGER *Main Risks:* * being ineffective * lack of direction * failing one's responsibilities
External to the Organization	*Influence Factors:* (+) credibility halo (+) perceived objectivity (+) freedom to experiment— not dependent on one job (−) need internal advocate (−) less information about system (−) must build trust (B) CONSULTANT *Main Risks:* * not reading internal climate right * not helping * being too much of an outsider	*Influence Factors:* (+) external legal powers (+) social support (−) little access or information (−) low trust within the system (D) REGULATORY AGENT *Main Risks:* * not getting access to the organization * misusing power * failing in mission

Controlling
Your Own Fate:
Role-Shaping

In this final chapter I not only review the major themes but bring together a number of points which have been scattered throughout the text. These points all aim at understanding the process for controlling your consultancy. The first and most important step is to accept that having technical expertise is not automatically the same thing as being able to help someone else deal with problems in this area. But recognizing the importance of the consulting process is an important step in this direction. Effective process is all the more important because consulting roles usually do not have the formal power of line positions, so that the consultant has to work in a variety of modes depending on the client and the particular situation.

This need for flexibility is also a source of the ambiguity which always goes with the territory. Consultants can manage this, however, through the ways in which they define client's expectations, as well as their own. It is particularly important that these expectations be negotiated early in a project, along with a process for changing expectations as the project progresses. Some of the toughest problems stem from unrecognized mismatches of expectations which we called problems in non-synchronization.

An internal consultant also needs to recognize and diagnose human system dynamics, as differentiated from the behavior of individuals. These system characteristics are both a context for the consultant and a target of the consultant's actions. We also considered the individual dimension, that is, the use of different modes of face-to-face influence: Rewards and Punishments, Participation and

Trust, Common Vision, and Assertive Persuasion. Each of these can be appropriate (or not) depending on personal style and the situation. An effective internal consultant generally needs to use more than one of these modes and to know when each is best.

We described some of the "dilemmas of doing business" as an internal helper. These included being a helper versus a controller, helping versus selling, doing versus learning, relaxing versus taking risks, and remaining mysterious versus sharing your "magic" with clients. These dilemmas are best dealt with if the consultant is conscious of daily choices, even those made unconsciously. Some specific, rather mundane skills are also helpful in dealing with these dilemmas: designing and managing meetings, diagnosing process problems, preparing and using reports, educating clients (as well as yourself), and being able to seek help and accept it from those around you. Finally we considered the advantages and disadvantages of external and internal consulting roles, with an emphasis on how to shape the internal role to obtain more of the strengths inherent in the typical external consultant's role.

Things to Watch Out For

Certain aspects of the typical internal consulting situation can block effectiveness unless recognized and managed. Some of these pitfalls are:

- Giving help whether someone wants it or not (or in such a way that you can't find out whether it is or isn't wanted);
- Conceding the role-shaping process to forces around you, instead of managing your own fate;
- Focusing too much on single events and not paying attention to influencing patterns;
- Being measured and evaluated by others' (professional or nonprofessional) standards and accepting them without any attempt to influence them;

- Developing a kind of arrogance toward your clients, such that you are no longer respecting, listening, learning, or adapting to their needs and situation;
- Becoming dependent on the technical logic of your efforts and ignoring the process by which things can actually be implemented;
- Starting a project by making unstated assumptions, thereby building in problems.

Themes

Our most obvious theme is that role expectations are never completely explicit. If the demands put on you by the client do not feel right, or if the client is behaving differently than you would like, then it's worth investigating and attempting to renegotiate expectations. The early contracting process is, then, crucial to success because it sets the stage. It's one of your best opportunities to discuss *how* you set and change role expectations as the project continues. The point is to define these alterations as part of "business as usual" rather than as a crisis. This renegotiation should feel like a natural and *effective* thing to do, not an automatic indication of failure. This attitude (nobody's perfect, and we should change as soon as we recognize the need) is probably the most important one to establish between client and consultant, since it influences what you will disclose to one another and whether you will be able to see patterns rather than just your own piece of the action.

A second theme was that there is no one "right" internal consultant role. Effective role definition depends on the client's needs and your own resources, and part of your basic task is to help the clients make conscious choices about the kinds of help they want. One simple model of roles was the expert, resource, and process distinction. A consultant may plan one or more of these roles with a client or may shift from one to the other over the course of a

project. For instance, an information systems consultant
may start in the expert mode, doing a specific project for the
client, then shift to a process focus to develop the client's
familiarity with on-line terminal use and self-programming
methods. With this development of the client's capacities,
the consultant can then serve as a periodic resource consultant, at the client's initiative. This contrasts with being
stuck in the expert mode where the client remains dependent
and is a constant energy drain on the consulting group. This
kind of evolution works best if it is openly discussed and
managed by consultant and client as a team. If it is left to
chance, there is no real test of whether the process is on
the track.

Another theme concerned the importance of thinking in systemic terms about how things happen in your own
group and in the organization. Your impact is partly a function of seeing what the client's issues are and when to make
an input that will help rather than exacerbate these issues.
In addition, there are power dynamics related to your group
(if you are part of a staff group); and part of your business
should be to pay attention to the choices made by unit
leaders. These choices include definition of mission, what
issues to deal with as a group, where to locate your offices,
whether to have offices at all, whom to inform about the
nature of your group's activities and outcomes, and when
to respond to client demands instead of doing internal
group business. It is the pattern of such choices, if they are
made consciously with an eye toward the group's role as a
consulting arm of the company, that can lead to significant
and long-term effect in the organization.

Many of the role-shaping activities I have been tout-
ing here are aimed at developing an effective *language*
about the internal consulting process. This language is useful in several ways. It helps you think about your own situations and problems and see patterns in what may have
previously felt like random events or personal failings.

Many of our frustrations come from being in the wrong role or in a role that's not well-defined. The language also helps you discuss experiences and problems with professional colleagues. It increases the likelihood that you will share observations about the process or the "hows" of what you're doing, in addition to the usual technical discussions. Staying current with the field, for an internal consultant, means learning new ways to share and apply your technical skills with clients, not just keeping up with the external field. Finally, the language of role-shaping is particularly useful in discussions with your client. It's worth a good bit of effort to develop this common language between you so that issues, problems, or changes in direction can be discussed directly and put into effect. Without a common view of mutual roles, it's hard to control your own fate. Each of you may feel that your problems are caused by the other, rather than (as is often the case) being the result of something awry in role definitions or the structure of the helping process.

Another theme is related to common language; its usefulness in creating structures (regular meetings, reports, informal discussions, rating sheets, or reports done by the client) that help you get information about your own impact and effect on the client system. One of the few truths in human behavior is that the *consequences* of our actions don't necessarily match our *intentions*. We learn by creating structures through which we determine regularly whether we are having different effects than we intended. If we expect to have this kind of information on a regular basis, we need to make it as easy as possible for them to give it to us, especially when they do not want to be critical. The easiest way to get feedback is to let it be known that you know you are not perfect and would like to hear about the effects your products and process are having.

This feedback process, plus built-in evaluation or checkpoints, allows regular role renegotiation if something is not right. These critiques should be seen as a piece of normal business, not a crisis.

After all of these considerations about how to perform in the internal consulting role, the basic question remains of whether you are in the right business. What is personally satisfying to you? How much certainty and security do you need? What facets of staff support work drive you crazy? What feels like growth and learning? Do you get that from this kind of organizational role? What would you be doing with your energy and expertise if you were not in an internal helping position? Do you have the option to switch to this? What would you have to do to make it happen?

These questions are not intended to send people out of internal consulting, but rather to clarify why they are in it and if the original reasons for getting involved are still valid. The ambiguity and multiple modes of indirect influence associated with internal consulting do not form the right work environment for many people. Recognizing that your needs have changed reflects our main theme: if we don't take the initiative to shape our work situations and roles as we would like them to be, it's unlikely that anyone else will. In that case, the expectations placed upon us will be a random collection of constraints rather than a chosen set of challenges.

Appendices

Exercises for Improving Control over the Role-Shaping Process

143

Appendix 1. Controlling Your Role as a Staff Group

As a means to taking more control of the role-shaping process for your staff group, it would be helpful to have a team meeting where you work on the following two areas:

Analyzing Group Role Control

- Have we agreed upon a mission statement? Is it subscribed to by the formal head of our group, high-level executives, and heads of the key client groups whom we serve?
- Who controls the scheduling of our time and energy? Is there a heavy influence that is outside our control?
- Can we say no to client requests? If not, why not?
- Do we set our role expectations or is it done somewhere else in the organization?
- Who sets our performance standards? Do we influence the evaluation processes for individuals and/or for the group? Are we evaluated as a team as well as individuals? Is this done fairly?
- Does the team share developmental goals? Do these goals include such areas as the helping process and role management?
- Do we schedule internal events just for our own development or benefit? Do we continue with our plans even when pressured to do something else on short notice?

- Can we publicize what we do and what we've done? Do we negotiate this freedom when we start a project with a new client group?

Exercising Group Role Control

- Do we set common group goals and review them periodically? (If so, list them and note which ones apply to all staff group members, which are selective. Be clear also about what the group as a whole is trying to accomplish and/or become.)
- How can we better publicize our philosophy, mission, values, or strengths? (Brainstorm items which can be referred to later.)
- Do we structure projects so that we have some flexibility in our roles? Identify some structures that will provide this flexibility (for example, a well-defined exploratory phase followed by explicit contracting).
- Do we stick to scheduled meetings with one another? If not, what sanctions do we employ to change that behavior?
- Do we challenge clients who demand immediate answers which are impossible to provide? Do we back each other up in trying to resist such inappropriate demands? Are there times when we undercut each other by being an alternative source for a simplistic request?
- Do we believe that it is worthwhile to exercise conscious role control as a staff group? If so, we should get together every six to eight weeks to review patterns, experiences, and opportunities in this area.

Appendix 2. Consultant-Client Role-Shaping

This exercise should be done by internal consultant(s) and client(s) who have contracted to work on a problem or project.

(1) Meet and do the following analysis (or review, if you have already worked out a basic mode of working):

- goals of the consultation
- indicators to measure degrees of success
- key consultant responsibilities
- key client responsibilities
- expectations regarding time allocations for different phases
- likely process problems
- how we will keep each other informed, and about what
- frequency with which we will check our progress

(2) Now, working separately, each of you answer the following questions:

- My main worries or fears about this project are...
- What I like most about the other person is....
- What I'd like to see more and less of from the other person....
- What issues do I feel I can't raise without causing problems or hurt feelings?
- The main constraints on me that I hope will be recognized by the other person are....
- What inappropriate expectations does the other person seem to have of me? Which ones do I dislike the most?

(3) Then, again as a group, exchange your answers.

(4) Follow this with recontracting:

- An amended set of expectations for each of us;
- A set of norms by which we will work, such as:

    our frequency of getting together;

    what we can talk about, what we want to avoid;

    what kinds of role expectations we want to re-negotiate easily;

    what we should keep confidential, what we feel free to share;

    who we should keep informed about our activities (and who will take responsibility for this);

    how we will deal with cost and budget issues.

(This exercise can be done one-to-one, or group-to-group if there is a consulting team working with a client group.)

Appendix 3.   Analyzing Your Role Ambiguity

Role ambiguity is a catch-all term for a number of vague experiences. People may be suffering from an overload of role ambiguity but never associate it with its label. Therefore, it helps to think about how ambiguity is affecting you and to recognize problem patterns before they get out of hand. The following questions help to analyze your own situation.

- How much role ambiguity do I experience in my present role?

very little				some				a great deal
1	2	3	4	5	6	7	8	9

- What aspects of my role are most clear; which most ambiguous?

Areas of Clarity	Areas of Ambiguity

- How much ambiguity do I generally like? At what point do I feel uncomfortable? Do I like the amount that I have now? Do I use that ambiguity to my own advantage?
- If I don't like my present level of ambiguity, how can I gain more clarity? What do I have to do to get others to be clearer with me? If I clarify client roles more, would my role also be clarified?

- What am I going to do about this, and when will I start? When will I repeat this analysis to see if I am making progress?
- Can I arrange a discussion with my fellow consultants where we share experiences and strategies about role ambiguity? Can we identify aspects of the way our staff group is structured or managed which contribute to excessive role ambiguity? If so, what do we have to do to change it, and who will take the first steps?

Appendix 4.   Staff Group Power: Analyzing the Factors That Block Our Ability to Make Things Happen

As a part of role clarification and project direction, staff groups should assess periodically the nature of the environment within which they work. It helps to do this in a team/group setting, since members, obviously, have different experiences which can enhance the overall picture.

In this assessment, a key area to describe is the pattern of obstacles which you face. The following exercise might be useful to you.

(1) Members of an internal consulting or staff group, meeting together, spend about one hour brainstorming about all the present factors in their organization (the larger parent system) that tend to reduce their power as a staff unit.

Consider:

- Structures
- Policies
- Our group's norms

- Reward system features
- Organizational norms
- Our physical location and layout

- Typical political games
- Our function's charter

After brainstorming (and visibly recording the list of factors on a board or newsprint), the group should use the list as the basis for three follow-up agenda items:

(2) Are there factors here which we could help to change? What would that require?

(3) Are there factors here that we can't do much about, but whose effects/blockages could be reduced if we changed how we respond to them? How do we want to respond differently in the future?

(4) Who else do we feel would benefit from a similar exercise? And whom do we want to share the results of this exercise with? When will we do this, and in what form?

Finally, when will we review whether we have had any impact on these factors, and when will we do a repeat assessment?

Index